ROBERT M. O'NEIL attended Harvard University where he received his B.A., an M.A. in American History, and a law degree. He served as Law Clerk to Mr. Justice William J. Brennan, Jr., United States Supreme Court, and has been a professor of law at the University of California, Berkeley, the University of Cincinnati, and the University of Indiana, where he also serves today as Vice President, Bloomington campus. He has written many books, including: *Discriminating Against Discrimination* (which discusses reverse discrimination in the historic DeFunis case); *The Judiciary in Vietnam; The Price of Dependency: Civil Liberties in the Welfare State; The Courts, The Government, and Higher Education; Free Speech: Responsible Communication Under The Law;* and *Civil Liberties: Case Studies and the Law.* He is currently a member of the Carnegie Foundation Council on Policy Studies in Higher Education, and he has written widely on the subject of the law concerning public employees.

Also in this Series

THE RIGHTS OF VETERANS	36285	$1.75
THE RIGHTS OF MENTAL PATIENTS	36574	$1.75
THE RIGHTS OF MILITARY PERSONNEL	33365	$1.50
THE RIGHTS OF YOUNG PEOPLE	31963	$1.50
THE RIGHTS OF ALIENS	31534	$1.50
THE RIGHTS OF STUDENTS	32045	$1.50
THE RIGHTS OF MENTALLY RETARDED PERSONS	31351	$1.50
THE RIGHTS OF CANDIDATES AND VOTERS	28159	$1.50
THE RIGHTS OF GAY PEOPLE	24976	$1.75
THE RIGHTS OF HOSPITAL PATIENTS	22459	$1.50
THE RIGHTS OF THE POOR	28001	$1.25
THE RIGHTS OF SUSPECTS	28043	$1.25
THE RIGHTS OF TEACHERS	25049	$1.50
THE RIGHTS OF WOMEN	27953	$1.75

Where better paperbacks are sold, or directly from the publisher. Include 25¢ per copy for mailing; allow three weeks for delivery.

Avon Books, Mail Order Dept., 250 West 55th Street, New York, N.Y. 10019

AN AMERICAN
CIVIL LIBERTIES
UNION HANDBOOK

THE
RIGHTS OF
GOVERNMENT
EMPLOYEES

THE BASIC ACLU
GUIDE TO A
GOVERNMENT
EMPLOYEES' RIGHTS

Robert O'Neil

General Editors of this series:
Norman Dorsen, *Chairperson*
Aryeh Neier, *Executive Director*

 A DISCUS BOOK/PUBLISHED BY AVON BOOKS

To Karen

THE RIGHTS OF GOVERNMENT EMPLOYEES is an original publication of Avon Books. This work has never before been published in book form.

AVON BOOKS
A division of
The Hearst Corporation
959 Eighth Avenue
New York, New York 10019

First Avon Printing, May, 1978

AVON TRADEMARK REG. U.S. PAT. OFF. AND IN
OTHER COUNTRIES, MARCA REGISTRADA, HECHO EN
U.S.A.

Printed in the U.S.A.

Acknowledgments

This book reflects the contributions of many people—too many to acknowledge properly here. I would like to give special recognition and appreciation to four Indiana University law students who, during the spring and summer of 1976, devoted many hours not only to research but also to analysis of the issues of public employment law. Michael Flanigan, Suzanne Matt O'Shea, Robert Parker and Steven Wagner formed a most effective research team, from whom I learned much as we did the initial work on this book. The process of preparing the manuscript was in the able and accurate hands of Donna Harbstreit, and the responsibilities of ensuring its safe custody, transmittal and revision were those of Norma Fox. To all these people I owe a special debt, and hope they share proper credit for the final product.

Contents

Preface

This guide sets forth your rights under present law and offers suggestions on how you can protect your rights. It is one of a continuing series of handbooks published in cooperation with the American Civil Liberties Union.

The hope surrounding these publications is that Americans informed of their rights will be encouraged to exercise them. Through their exercise, rights are given life. If they are rarely used, they may be forgotten and violations may become routine.

This guide offers no assurances that your rights will be respected. The laws may change and, in some of the subjects covered in these pages, they change quite rapidly. An effort has been made to note those parts of the law where movement is taking place but it is not always possible to predict accurately when the law *will* change.

Even if the laws remain the same, interpretations of them by courts and administrative officials often vary. In a federal system such as ours, there is a built-in problem of the differences between state and federal law, not to speak of the confusion of the differences from state to state. In addition, there are wide variations in the ways in which particular courts and administrative officials will interpret the same law at any given moment.

If you encounter what you consider to be a specific abuse of your rights you should seek legal assistance. There are a number of agencies that may help you, among them ACLU affiliate offices, but bear in mind that the ACLU is a limited-purpose organization. In many communities, there are federally funded legal service offices which provide assistance to poor persons who cannot afford the costs of legal representation. In general, the rights that the ACLU defends are freedom of inquiry and expression; due process of law; equal protection of the laws; and privacy. The authors in this series have discussed other rights in these books (even though they sometimes fall outside the ACLU's usual concern) in order to provide as much guidance as possible.

These books have been planned as guides for the people directly affected: therefore the question and answer format. In some of these areas there are more detailed works available for "experts." These guides seek to raise the largest issues and inform the non-specialist of the basic law on the subject. The authors of the books are themselves specialists who understand the need for information at "street level."

No attorney can be an expert in every part of the law. If you encounter a specific legal problem in an area discussed in one of these handbooks, show the book to your attorney. Of course, an attorney will not be able to rely *exclusively* on the handbook to provide you with adequate representation. But if she or he hasn't had a great deal of experience in the specific area, the handbook can provide helpful suggestions on how to *proceed*.

Norman Dorsen, Chairperson
American Civil Liberties Union

Aryeh Neier, Executive Director
American Civil Liberties Union

The principal purpose of these handbooks is to inform individuals of their rights. The authors from time to time suggest what the law should be. When this is done, the views expressed are not necessarily those of the American Civil Liberties Union.

Introduction

A decade ago a book about the law of public employment could not have been written. There were cases, to be sure, dealing with loyalty oaths and a few other issues of importance to persons who worked in the public sector. But there was no coherent body of law defining comprehensively the rights of such people. The differences between public and private employees' rights were obvious, and the need for judicial review of those differences could not long be deferred. Moreover, by the early 1970s most other classes of government beneficiaries—welfare recipients, public housing tenants, subsidy claimants, state college students and others—had been to court and had come away with at least some victories. Thus the development of a meaningful body of public employment law was inevitable.

The course of this development has been uneven. Major strides have been made in protecting public workers from discrimination on grounds of race and sex (although women have fared less well than minorities). Persons with physical handicaps and older workers have also received substantial protection, more from legislatures than from the courts. The zone of privacy within which a government employee is free of special constraints during evening and weekend time has considerably expanded, although troublesome intrusions remain. The ability of government workers to express freely and publicly their views, even about policies of the agencies for which they work, has received some protection from the courts—although the status of the "whistle blower" is far from clear, as recent cases have shown us. And the ability of federal workers to take part in politics is still severely curtailed, so long as the Hatch Act remains in force.

It is the procedural rights of government employees that have fared least well. Courts have generally declined to extend to public workers the procedures—mainly the right to a hearing before termination—that other government beneficiaries now enjoy. Supreme Court decisions have been quite explicit in drawing that distinction, suggesting that people who work for the government can afford (as welfare clients, students, tenants and others cannot) to press their claim after the relationship has ended. Since employment means livelihood for all workers, and since many who work for the government are barely above the subsistence level even when fully employed, the distinction seems insensitive. Yet there is little likelihood that public employees' procedural rights will ever match those of other government beneficiaries.

The purpose of this book is to describe the current state of the law. Others have done much to change the law and to advocate and enact reform. Many organizations are dedicated to the interests of public employees in general, or to particular groups (such as teachers in the public schools or faculty members at state colleges and universities). Readers who encounter particular problems under agency policies should consult such organizations. I hope that the material in this book will provide general background and will outline the kinds of rights that may be asserted with some estimate of the probability of success. Much remains to be done in this field, though we have come a considerable distance in the last ten or fifteen years.

Robert M. O'Neil

January, 1978

I

Public Employment and Individual Rights: An Overview

May a government agency deny a person a job for any reason at all?

No. Any public agency that employs people must consider each applicant on the basis of his or her qualifications. A government job may not be denied on grounds of race, sex, or religion. For most jobs, political affiliation may no longer be used as a standard. It is true that a person does not have an absolute constitutional right to government employment in general or to a particular position. But that does not mean that applications may be rejected, or employees discharged, for arbitrary or discriminatory reasons.[1] Most of this book is devoted to describing the standards that may and may not be applied to test eligibility for public employment.

There once was a time when government agencies could hire or fire people pretty much at the whim of the supervisor or for purely personal reasons. In 1892, Mr. Justice Oliver Wendell Holmes (then a Massachusetts state court judge) said that "a man may have a right to talk politics, but not to be a policeman," and went on to hold that an officer could be fired for his partisan activity.[2] As late as 1952, the U.S. Supreme

Court held that public school teachers who objected to signing a loyalty oath were "at liberty to take their beliefs and associations and go elsewhere" if they did not "choose to work on such terms."[3]

Now the law has changed considerably, and courts no longer dismiss the claims of public employees in this casual fashion. As the result of many decisions in the late 1960s and 1970s, new principles protecting government workers have emerged. The Supreme Court has recently said that "public employment . . . may not be conditioned upon the surrender of constitutional rights which could not be abridged by direct government action."[4] This new body of law reflects a growing concern for the rights of all people who seek benefits or receive support from the government—welfare recipients, state university students, tenants in public housing projects, and others. The courts have also recognized that government controls most of the jobs in a growing number of fields, so that a restriction on *public* employment may effectively keep a person out of *all* employment. While teachers, security officers, nurses, bus drivers, and others can still find private jobs, the nonpublic sector is shrinking, and the options outside government employment have diminished proportionately.

Do public employees enjoy the same rights and liberties as people who work in the private sector?

As a result of recent changes in the law, public employees today enjoy *most* (though not quite all) of the rights and liberties of general citizenship. Courts have, however, stopped short of holding that people who work for government retain every right. Specific limitations and restrictions have been upheld even though they would not be valid if applied to other citizens. For example, people who work for the federal government may not take as active a role in partisan politics as other citizens may.[5] Municipal employees may be required to live within the city limits.[6] Certain special grooming and dress requirements have been upheld.[7] People may be denied public employment for certain forms of private sexual conduct.[8] Applicants for government jobs may be required to disclose certain information not available through the census.[9] Most of this book will be devoted to the presentation, explanation, and application of these limitations.

Do all public employees have the same rights and liberties?

The scope of legal protection depends in part on the nature of the job. Military personnel, for example, have fewer rights than other people who work for the government. (In fact, the situation in the military service is so different from civilian employment that we will not consider it in this book. A companion volume, *The Rights of Military Personnel*,[10] is devoted entirely to that topic.) Even in the civilian sector, there are significant differences between agencies and even between jobs. Some restrictions have been upheld for the police and fire departments that would not be sustained where the need for uniformity and discipline is less clear. On the other hand, groups such as state university faculty members may enjoy greater rights than other public employees because of the sensitive nature of teaching and scholarship.

Even within the rank and file of public personnel, the range of rights will vary with the length and particular nature of a person's work. For example, an overweight gym teacher presents a quite different problem from an overweight telephone operator or file clerk. We may tolerate a former drug addict as a custodian when we would be uneasy about having such a person as an air traffic controller. The courts have begun to recognize these distinctions; they tend to appraise more closely the relationship between the particular position and the particular restriction, rather than ruling that a restriction must be valid or invalid for all purposes. But the specification is far from complete. We will encounter many instances in which conditions and restrictions are ruled on with little recognition of the wide variety of government jobs.

Which laws define the rights of public employees?

Certain basic protections come from the Constitution. Freedoms of speech, association, and religion, and due process of law are guaranteed by the federal Constitution and by the constitutions of most states. In addition, the provisions of the federal Bill of Rights now apply to all state and local government employment practices just as forcefully as they apply to the federal civil service. In many areas, statutes (acts of Congress or of a state legislature) have extended or refined the constitutional guarantees. Perhaps the most obvious illustration is in the area of discrimination, where Title VII of the 1964 Civil Rights Act was recently amended to cover most public as well as private employment. The basis of this law is the rights of equality guaranteed by the Constitution, but the statute is more specific than the Constitution and provides remedies that would not otherwise exist for aggrieved employees. Certain laws protecting workers simply apply alike to public and private employment, without drawing any distinction. Still other laws refer specifically to public workers, although they may have counterparts on the private side. These laws may and often do go beyond, or *add to,* what the Constitution ensures, but they *may not take away* anything that is guaranteed by the Bill of Rights.

In some areas, the laws affecting public employment vary widely. Collective bargaining provides a good illustration. The Constitution guarantees only that government workers may not be discharged for joining a union. Some state laws go quite far in requiring government agencies to bargain with employee unions, and even give public workers the right to strike. In these states, there is little difference between the union rights of public and private workers, although they come from quite different laws. Other states make no provision for public employee collective bargaining and union contracts may even be illegal. (In fact, collective bargaining does exist unofficially in most such states, and contracts are signed.) In a third group of states, and in the federal civil service, provision has been made for limited bargaining or negotiation, but the strike is still illegal and union rights are more limited than in the private sector. With these wide differences, it is not possible to give a comprehensive answer to questions such as "May a public employee go out on strike?" or "May a public employee union bargain collectively on behalf of its members?" The answer must be a cautious "That depends" or "The situation varies considerably from state to state." In almost every area where the Constitution does not define the full scope of government employees' rights, you must know the terms of the local law. The most we can do in this book is to identify the variations and outline their general dimensions.

Do employees of private business enjoy similar rights?

Since the subject of this book is *public* employment, the question is beyond its scope. But a few words about private employment may be helpful. Many of the rights guaranteed by legislation apply similarly to public and private workers. In other areas (for example, the right to bargain collectively and to strike against the employer), private employees are better protected than are their public counterparts. Other special laws apply only to public employment and are thus of no avail to those in private business and industry.

But what of the Constitution? The simple rule is that the guarantees of the Bill of Rights do not apply at all in the private sector. But some employers are so extensively involved with the government, or (like some public utilities or major political parties) they exercise such essentially governmental functions that they are treated as though they were public. A restaurant in a publicly owned and operated parking garage, for example, is bound by the Constitution even though it is under private ownership. Certain private colleges and universities that depend heavily on the government for support have been held bound by the Constitution in their employment practices. But the percentage of private employment affected in this way is quite small. You should not assume that simply because a company is licensed by or does business with the government, the Constitution automatically controls its personnel practices.

Do applicants for public employment have legal rights?

Many of the cases defining the rights of public employees were brought by people who were seeking, rather than those who already held, government jobs. Thus applicants clearly do enjoy many of the same rights as do incumbents. There are some differences, however, mainly in the area of procedures and remedies. Often a statute will give protection to a person who has been employed for a certain period; such protection is clearly unavailable to an applicant. When it comes to the Constitution, the basic rule is that a person may not be denied a job for a reason that would not support a discharge. But the *applicant* may be less well able than the *incumbent* to prove a constitutional violation. Rarely, for example, does an applicant have the kind of legal interest that requires a hearing following the denial of employment. Thus, while the basic substantive rights are similar, important differences exist in the ways these rights may be enforced.

Do the rights of public employees apply off as well as on the job?

Surprisingly, there is very little law on the scope of public employees' private rights. Much of the controversy over restrictions on political activity falls into this area, for government workers have claimed that they should be able to use their free time for partisan campaigning. Most of the cases defining the relationship between public employment and sexual contacts (both homosexual and heterosexual) have involved off-the-job liaisons. There have been intriguing cases of employees who belonged to nudist camps, lived on communal farms, or engaged in weekend orgies. The results in these cases have varied widely; the emerging principles will be discussed in Chapter V. The courts have not, however, stated clearly where the line falls between the "public" and the "private" life of the government worker. The answers are easy only at the extremes. On the one hand, everyone assumes that a weekend overtime parking violation will not jeopardize even a police officer's job. At the other extreme, a murder conviction is likely to cause any public employee a great deal of difficulty. The hard cases lie between these two poles—certain types of theft, but not all thefts, will disqualify a person for some kinds of jobs. It would be impossible to list all the offenses or activities off the job that may have some bearing on a public employee's position—if only because the very first test case would doubtless involve conduct no one had thought of during the drafting process. What is needed is a general standard defining the relationship between public employment and off-the-job conduct—a standard the courts have thus far failed to provide. For this reason, we can give no definite or even helpful answer to this perfectly proper question.

May a public employee be forced to violate the rights of other people?

In general, no. There are very few cases on this issue. A decade ago, the California Supreme Court held that a social worker could not be fired for refusing to take part in a "midnight raid" that involved unannounced entry into the homes of welfare clients. The social worker objected to the raid because he felt it would require him to violate the privacy of poor people he was supposed to be helping. The California high court ordered his reinstatement, after finding that the raids were indeed unconstitutional, and added that a government employee could not be forced to violate the constitutional rights and liberties of others as a condition of employment.[11]

A more recent Michigan case involved a similar issue. A Detroit police officer was dismissed because she refused to pose as a prostitute, or decoy. She claimed that such work was not only dangerous and demeaning, but violated the legal rights of men who would be solicited. "I thought," she later commented, "it was clearly entrapment." When she appealed the loss of her job, an arbitration panel ordered her reinstatement, with full seniority and back pay.[12] This decision strongly implied that a public employee may not be required to violate the constitutional rights of other people. While these two cases are consistent, there are few other precedents.

What should a person do if he or she is denied employment on a seemingly improper ground?

The first step is to ascertain as clearly as possible the reason for the rejection. (This does not mean that the *stated* reason will always be the *real* reason; cases are legion in which women and minorities have been denied employment on grounds such as "experience" or "qualification" when in fact a more sinister motive was operative.) When the reason is identified (through the employer's acknowledgment or the employee's belief), a remedy may become apparent. If, for example, you believe you have been rejected for reasons of sex or race (or both), it may be possible to file a grievance with a local or state antidiscrimination agency. Such a complaint may also be taken to the federal Equal Employment Opportunity Commission, although the state or local agency should be tried first. (In Chapter VI, the functions of such agencies are described more fully.)

If the basis for the rejection is not one of these forms of discrimination, the next step is less clear. If, for example, you have been denied public employment because of a political association or belief, or on the basis of a controversial speech or article, such action may be clearly illegal but can only be corrected by a court. (Of course, every effort should first be made to persuade the agency that it has acted wrongly; going to court is expensive, time-consuming, and should be a last resort.) Such cases may be handled by an organization that has concern for the rights of public employees. The various legal services' offices and programs may help if you cannot afford to hire a lawyer. If you do have money, you would be expected to retain counsel. Often a list of available attorneys can be obtained from the local bar association referral service, which is typically listed in the local telephone directory. These and other avenues should lead you to someone who can at least provide sound advice, and can help you to seek redress where appropriate.

What should a public employee do if dismissed for a seemingly improper reason?

The status of the public employee who loses his or her job is somewhat different from that of the unsuccessful applicant. Sometimes there will be an established grievance procedure, which should of course be followed first. Courts will usually refuse to consider a lawsuit if the discharged employee failed to pursue any remedies available within the agency—even if the agency procedure appears cumbersome, unfair, or time-consuming. Sometimes the matter may be resolved through the grievance channel, especially if it was the result of a mistake or misunderstanding. If an internal appeal does not bring satisfaction, the employee may then seek outside recourse in much the same way as the rejected applicant. Where the discharge involved discrimination on grounds of race, religion, sex, age, or national origin (and sometimes physical handicap), the employee may seek external administrative review as soon as the internal procedures have been exhausted. Dismissal on other grounds may require the aid of a voluntary organization, or an attorney, or both, in much the same way we suggested for the rejected applicant.

What relief is available to a wronged applicant or employee?

The most obvious remedy for a wrongful denial of employment or a wrongful dismissal is to order the agency to hire (or rehire) the aggrieved person. Courts may also order the payment of money damages to a person who has been wronged, through loss of earnings, injury to professional reputation or opportunity, etc. In extreme cases, where bad faith has been proved, damages going well beyond actual injury (so-called punitive damages) may also be awarded. Occasionally, a court may direct the agency to remove from the files any reference to the matter, in order to protect the employee's or applicant's reputation and future employment opportunities. But the basic remedy is to get (or get back) the job in question, and this is the relief most commonly decreed.

NOTES

1. Cases which are not fully cited in this chapter will be discussed (and fully cited) in the later, substantive chapters.
2. *McAuliffe v. Mayor and Board of Aldermen,* 155 Mass. 216, 29 N.E. 517 (1892).
3. *Adler v. Board of Education,* 342 U.S. 485, 492 (1952).
4. *Keyishian v. Board of Regents,* 385 U.S. 589, 605–06 (1967).
5. *United States Civil Service Commission v. Letter Carriers,* 413 U.S. 548 (1973).
6. *McCarthy v. Philadelphia Civil Service Commission,* 424 U.S. 645 (1976).
7. *Kelley v. Johnson,* 425 U.S. 238 (1976).

8. *Pettit v. State Board of Education*, 109 Cal. Rptr. 665, 513 P.2d 889 (1973).
9. *County of Nevada v. McMillen*, 114 Cal. Rptr. 345, 522 P.2d 1345 (1974).
10. The title of the first edition is *The Rights of Servicemen*; the title indicated here is the one projected for the second edition.
11. *Parrish v. Civil Service Commission*, 66 Cal. 2d 60, 425 P.2d 223, 57 Cal. Rptr. 623 (1967).
12. *Detroit News*, July 23, 1976, p. 1-F, col. 1.

II

Initial Qualifications for Public Employment

There can be a "catch-22" quality about seeking a government job. Consider the unhappy case of Thomas L. Fox, Jr., a Washington, D.C., resident who wanted to be a fireman. When he applied for a position in the Fire Department, he was rejected because he was too short; the minimum height was 5'7" and Fox was only 5'6½". With the help of the American Civil Liberties Union, Fox went to court to challenge the height rule. He won his case and went back to the Fire Department—only to discover that he was now too old— several years over the maximum age (29) by which firemen must be initially hired.[1] His victory was a rather hollow triumph, although others would benefit from his perseverance. The *Fox* case illustrates the main theme of this chapter—that a person may encounter many obstacles in seeking a government job, even though the application and hiring process are usually routine.

Most government positions require some type of skill or experience. A law degree is routinely required for professional members of an attorney general's staff, and a truck driver must have a driver's license and some familiarity with large vehicles. These qualifications pose few legal problems, at least where they are genuine in purpose and uniform in application. As we will see, however, such seemingly neutral requirements may occasionally exclude disproportionate numbers of particular groups. And even where they may have general validity, they may also overlook the special qualifications of individual applicants. Certain conditions or restrictions on public employment—for example, the requirement that municipal workers live within the city limits—may relate only indirectly if at all to particular job responsibilities. In this chapter, we will examine many different kinds of restrictions and qualifications—concerning citizenship, residence, age, physical condition (including height and weight), physical disabilities, and past criminal conduct.

May U.S. citizenship be required for state and local government employment?

Not as a general rule. Several years ago, the U.S. Supreme Court reversed an old precedent[2] and held that states, counties, and cities could no longer deny employment to lawfully resident aliens.[3] A New York law had long forbidden the hiring of any aliens in the classified civil service. This law was challenged as a denial of equal protection under the Fourteenth Amendment of the U.S. Constitution. (The benefit of the equal protection clause extends to aliens as well as to citizens.) New York argued that such a requirement was necessary to ensure the loyalty of its civil servants, served to limit public benefits to those who were most closely identified with the government, and ensured long-term service since aliens might leave the country.

The Supreme Court rejected all three arguments in *Sugarman v. Dougall*[4] and held the New York law unconstitutional. While the Court recognized that a state might exclude certain groups of aliens from particularly sensitive government jobs, that could only be

done through "means . . . precisely drawn in light of
the acknowledged purpose." Not only had New York
failed to use such narrow tests; in fact, it had exempted
from the citizenship test particular government jobs
that appeared more sensitive and strategic than those
to which the ban applied. The Court left open the possibility that a state might "in an appropriately defined
class of positions, require citizenship as a qualification
for office."[5] The opinion concluded by recognizing that
"a restriction on the employment of noncitizens, narrowly confined, could have particular relevance to . . .
important state responsibility, for alienage itself is a
factor that reasonably could be employed in defining
'political community.' "[6]

The scope of the exception left open by the Supreme
Court remains to be defined. In July 1976, a three-
judge federal court upheld a New York law that requires that all state troopers be U.S. citizens.[7] The
court found that citizenship was specifically related to
the responsibilities of state law enforcement and was
thus a valid condition. About the same time, however,
another federal district court struck down New York's
citizenship requirement for public school teachers.[8]
This court found the ban on alien teachers excessively
broad, and at best loosely related to any valid state interest in the educational system. The Supreme Court
has agreed to review both cases during its 1977-78
term. Meanwhile, a federal court in California reached
the opposite conclusion regarding citizenship as a condition for police service.[9] Several states have recently
enacted laws barring citizenship requirements for public employment and other benefits.[10] The Supreme
Court, while not passing precisely on these issues, did
hold in the spring of 1977 that New York could not
deny financial aid to college students who were otherwise eligible simply because they were not U.S. citizens.[11]

May citizenship be required for federal civil service positions?

The answer is not clear. Since the beginning of the federal civil service system in 1883, aliens had been barred from classified federal positions. Over the years, there have been occasional challenges to that rule, but until recently they have been unsuccessful. In June 1976, the Supreme Court decided the case of *Hampton v. Mow Sun Wong*[12] in favor of five lawfully resident aliens who had been denied federal employment in San Francisco. However, the court rested its decision on a rather narrow ground. It did not hold that the federal government might not limit civil service positions to U.S. citizens, but only that the Civil Service Commission had tried to do so in the wrong way. Because of the highly sensitive nature of immigration and naturalization, decisions about the status of aliens are usually made by Congress or by the President. Although both were obviously aware of the Civil Service Commission's ban, there had never been any approval by higher authorities. The commission had simply adopted the restriction, without any sort of hearing or statement of special civil service interests. The Court now held that this action denied due process to resident aliens. Here too the Court reserved the larger issues for another day—whether (1) such a ban could be imposed by presidential or congressional action, and (2) whether the Civil Service Commission could itself adopt such a restriction by using better procedures.

After the Supreme Court decision, the President by executive order amended the Civil Service rules to exclude aliens from the civil service, except in limited circumstances where their employment might be necessary. After a new hearing on the original case in March 1977, the district court held that this order was valid and consistent with the Supreme Court's view. The delegated authority had now been properly exercised, in a way that the Constitution did not prevent.[13]

Do these decisions affect the rights of illegal aliens?

Probably not. The Supreme Court has stressed in the recent cases that the aliens involved were lawful residents. Illegal aliens are subject to deportation, a condition that would certainly undercut the state's interest in stability and continuity of employment. Moreover, the Supreme Court held in February 1976 that states may forbid private employers to hire illegal aliens if such hiring would make it harder for lawful resident workers to obtain jobs.[14] There is one possible complication: The Supreme Court held in 1974 that Mexicans and Canadians may commute freely into the United States to work, either on a daily or a seasonal basis, regardless of the employment situation in this country or of their intention to keep a permanent foreign residence.[15] Border commuters thus become lawfully, if temporarily, resident aliens, and may be able to claim the protection of the two decisions discussed earlier. It does seem, though, that public employment could perhaps be limited to citizens and aliens who have established a permanent residence in the United States.

May citizens be given a preference in public employment?

None of the relevant Supreme Court cases decided this issue. A preference for citizens might be valid where an absolute bar against aliens is invalid. This would be particularly likely if the state law spelled out strong interests underlying the preference. In the *Sugarman* case, however, the Supreme Court rejected New York's desire to favor citizens in allocating scarce resources. The Court quoted from an earlier decision involving aliens' rights, which stated that "justification of limiting expenses is particularly inappropriate and unreasonable when the discriminated class consists of aliens."[16] Quite recently, a federal district court held unconstitutional another New York law, which gave preference to citizens in public works project (a form of public employment). The court warned that "a state has a duty to all its lawful residents, resident alien or citizen," so that all applicants must be treated alike in a state-financed program to combat unemployment.[17] This decision was affirmed by the Supreme Court early in 1977.[18]

May a city employee be required to live within the city limits?

Yes. The Supreme Court has recently given an affirmative answer to this increasingly important question. Municipal practice varies widely; New York City, for example, once required its employees to live in the city, but repealed the law in 1962. Many other cities have made local residence a condition of employment, while others have not. Such requirements were challenged recently on the ground that they abridged the constitutional right of public employees to travel freely. The challengers relied on earlier Supreme Court decisions striking down laws that forced newcomers to wait a certain time before being eligible to vote, receive welfare, or practice certain professions. The Court had ruled that such laws unconstitutionally discriminated between newcomers and longer-term residents.

When it came to the residence of public employees, however, the Supreme Court took a different view. In a brief opinion in March 1976, the Supreme Court held that a Philadelphia fireman named McCarthy could be dismissed because he had moved away from the city. Previous decisions had "differentiated between a requirement of continuing residency and a requirement of prior residency of a given duration." In the welfare residence case, the Court said that "the residence requirement and the one-year waiting period requirement are distinct and independent prerequisites."[19] The earlier cases had also left open the "validity of appropriately defined and uniformly applied bona fide residence requirements."[20] Since the *McCarthy* case involved just such a residence requirement, the dismissal of the employee was sustained.

Although the Supreme Court did not elaborate, other cases have identified the special interests that such laws may serve. Several months earlier, the federal court of appeals sustained the rule requiring Cincinnati public school teachers to live within the city.[21] Such a condition, said that court, may serve several valid governmental objectives with respect to the city work force: a commitment to an urban school system, closer involvement in the welfare of the city government, greater degree of contact and familiarity with urban problems, and a higher degree of racial integration in the work force itself (since the proportion of minorities is invariably higher in the central city population than in the population of the adjacent suburbs). It is true that such a rule does restrict rather sharply the choices of certain people—both those living outside the city who seek municipal employment, and those already employed by the city who may wish to move to the suburbs. Such individual interests are substantial but, the Supreme Court has now held, do not outweigh the city's interests outlined earlier.

May a city impose a waiting period for public employment?

Probably not, although the Supreme Court has not ruled on this question. The distinction drawn in the *McCarthy* case between the requirement of actual residence and the waiting period struck down in other contexts suggests that a durational restriction would fare no better here. Such a waiting period distinguishes between two classes of residents solely on the basis of time of arrival. Unless the city can show strong interests that are served by such a waiting period—or unless public employment is less important than welfare benefits, voting, and medical care—the waiting period would probably be held invalid.

May a city give preference in employment to longer-term residents?

A preference may well present a different question from an absolute prohibition. Before the *McCarthy* decision, the Massachusetts Supreme Judicial Court held that a town could give priority in its employment policies to people who had resided there for a year or more, even though newcomers were not completely barred.[22] Since such a preference could be overcome in particular cases, and since cities and towns did show a plausible interest in preferring longer-term residents, the court reached a different conclusion. Presumably this judgment has gained additional support from the *McCarthy* decision, since the validity of residence requirements was in doubt at the time of the Massachusetts case.

May a public employee be forced to retire at a certain age?

Under the Constitution, yes. Mandatory retirement ages exist for virtually all public jobs. In most instances, retirement becomes compulsory at 60, 65, or even at 70—ages that correlate with a decline in strength, agility, and other qualities needed in a public worker. Several times, the Supreme Court has summarily affirmed decisions of lower courts upholding retirement ages.[23] A somewhat different case was presented, however, by Officer Robert Murgia, who was forced to retire from the Massachusetts state police force at age 50. Since he was in perfect health and anxious to continue working, Murgia brought suit challenging the constitutionality of the law. A federal district court struck down the 50-year retirement rule, finding it arbitrary in relation to the valid state interest in having healthy and alert police officers.[24] Not only was Murgia himself in perfect health, but there was evidence that other officers in their late forties were actually healthier than colleagues in their early forties.

The Supreme Court disagreed with the lower court and found that the Massachusetts rule rationally served the state's interest in a healthy state police force.[25] Although there may be exceptions, medical evidence showed that people do become more susceptible to heart attacks and other disabilities with increasing age. Identifying the exceptions (among whom Murgia might well be one) would be costly and time-consuming. Since the relationship between the rule and the governmental interest need only be "rational" and not a perfect fit, the existence of better alternatives was not critical. In the course of this decision—significant far beyond the narrow legal issue—the Court redefined the constitutional status of public employment: "This Court's decisions give no support to the proposition that a right of government employment per se is fundamental."[26] The meaning of this statement requires brief explanation. Where certain "fundamental" interests are involved—for example, the right to travel from state to state, or to vote—any restrictions are to be tested by a standard of "strict scrutiny."[27] In all other contexts, a merely "rational basis" will suffice. There was little doubt that the 50-year retirement rule would not have passed "strict scrutiny" had the interest in public employment been deemed "fundamental." But since the individual interest was not a "fundamental" one, a much looser nexus between the interest and the classification—between officers over and under 50—was acceptable.

May a government agency refuse to hire people over a certain age?

As a matter of constitutional law, there is no clear precedent. In the *Murgia* case, the court had no occasion to consider another part of the Massachusetts law, which limited initial eligibility for the state police to persons between the ages of 25 and 30. Government occupations that have early retirement rules typically also have upper-entry levels for initial employment.

There has been no separate constitutional test of such limits. Under the *Murgia* decision, however, it would seem that if the retirement part of the law is constitutionally valid, the same reasoning would apply to sustain the upper-entry. If a police officer is too old to be reliable at age 50, then presumably a state may decide that only persons under 30 can be trusted for rookie training—or that the state's investment in a police officer is so large that service less than 20 years will not bear adequate return. Whatever the reason, the *Murgia* case almost certainly validates such upper-entry limits.[28]

What protection is given by the Age Discrimination in Employment Act?

The *Murgia* decision was limited to constitutional issues. There is an important statute in the picture—the Age Discrimination in Employment Act, adopted by Congress in 1967 to protect the employment rights of persons between the ages of 40 and 65.[29] Until 1974, the law applied only to private employers, but a recent amendment extended its provisions to federal, state, and local government workers as well. It is too early to tell to what extent this law affects mandatory retirement policies of government agencies, although there are a few analogous cases involving private employers. The law creates an exception for any age limit that is a "bona fide occupational qualification," without defining that term.[30] One case suggests that where the reason for refusing to hire older people (or for imposing an unusually early retirement age) relates to the safety of other people (e.g., airline or bus passengers), an age limit is valid.[31] Another exception permits an employer to observe the terms of a seniority system or benefit plan "such as a retirement, pension or insurance plan which is not a subterfuge to evade the purposes of this law."[32] The Secretary of Labor has interpreted this proviso as a basis for validating all mandatory retirement systems that are uniformly applied as a part of pension systems. In December 1977 the Supreme Court held that a private employer could, under this provision, require workers to retire at age 60 pursuant to a bona fide retirement program that had been adopted in 1941. The court concluded that employers need not demonstrate a business or economic purpose to justify such plans which predated the Age Discrimination Act.[33]

The first public employment case to raise the mandatory retirement issue under the Age Discrimination in Employment Act reached a different result, however. In May 1976, a federal district court in Arkansas held that a city's 62-year retirement rule for firemen violated the Age Discrimination in Employment Act, since the city had shown no "special relevance" of that particular age in a fireman's life.[34] The city argued simply that firefighting was a hazardous occupation, and that risks to younger firemen as well as to senior officers justified the early retirement rule. But the court was unimpressed: "In the age bracket with which we are here concerned, there is no suggestion that the legitimate apprehensions of the city and the Fire Department cannot be met through periodic physical examinations." Thus the retirement rule in question— which would surely have survived constitutional challenge under *Murgia*—was held in violation of the Age Discrimination in Employment Act. This case opens a whole new chapter in the rights of older public workers. Clearly, the courts are not the only places where such rights may be vindicated.

The Age Discrimination Act provides remedies such as reinstatement to persons who have been unlawfully denied employment because of age. It is not yet clear whether additional damages for pain and suffering may be recovered; the courts appear to be split on that issue in the early cases. A district court in New Jersey awarded such damages, but was reversed by the court of appeals that feared possible abuses of the remedy, and felt conciliation would be aided by limiting the recoverable damages.[35] Later a district court in Illinois reached a different view, and the issue of the extent of damages is now very open.[36]

Congress has recently amended the Age Discrimination Act in a vitally important way, increasing protection from 65 to 70 for most public employees.[37]

During the fall of 1977 both houses of Congress were moving toward amendments which would raise the permissible retirement age. Since differences remained between the two versions the session adjourned without action. The House bill, the more sweeping of the two, would have eliminated any mandatory retirement age for federal employees and would have raised from 65 to 70 the age for employees in the private sector covered by the Act. Meanwhile, several states have eliminated mandatory retirement policies for their civil servants.[37]

May a person be denied employment because he or she is too young?

Many government occupations require that a person attain a certain age to be eligible. In states where the age of majority has been lowered to 18, a substantial group of new adults may be denied access to public employment. In one case that has considered this issue, the Supreme Court of New Jersey held that the 21-year requirement of a city police force had been superseded by the lowering of the age of majority.[38] This decision simply interpreted New Jersey laws, and might or might not be followed in other states. The Constitution does not require that all aspects of adulthood go together, though the New Jersey decision is persuasive in terms of the legislature's probable intent in making 18-year-olds generally eligible for civic rights and responsibilities.

May an applicant be required to meet minimum height and weight standards?

The Supreme Court ruled in 1977 that such standards are invalid unless the employer can demonstrate that they bear a direct relationship to ability to perform the job. Thus the Court struck down an Alabama law requiring that state prison guards be at least 5'2" and weigh at least 120 pounds, since the effect of that law was to exclude disproportionate numbers of women for reasons not essential to the job. But the court upheld a state rule which barred women from "contact" jobs in maximum security, all-male penitentiaries.[39] This decision seems to end the use of arbitrary height-weight eligibility standards, and thus opens many jobs in police, fire, and other public agencies to women.

Even before the Supreme Court spoke, many agencies were already eliminating or modifying height and weight minimums that were established years ago with the average white Anglo male applicant in mind, but that fit other applicants less well. Notably, the U.S. Civil Service Commission has ruled invalid both the height and weight rules for the National Park Police, in the absence of any scientific proof of the relationship between such criteria and the demands of the job.[40]

May an applicant be rejected for being overweight?

The answer may depend on the job for which the person applies. Clearly, excess weight is disabling in certain occupations—as witness the recent escape of a 150-pound convict from the custody of a 215-pound Detroit policeman who was unable to give chase.[41] Yet a California court held that even a physical education teacher, otherwise competent, could not be discharged solely for excessive weight without proof that her condition significantly impaired her ability to teach.[42] Similarly, a New York court reversed the denial of a license to an overweight teacher on the ground that "obesity, standing alone, is not reasonably and rationally related to the ability to teach or to maintain discipline."[43]

These decisions are not based on the Constitution, but rather reflect state court interpretations of state law. There is, in fact, a strong inference that the Constitution does not extend this far. A Florida court upheld the dismissal of an overweight fire department telephone operator, without regard for the job-relatedness of the weight rule, and the U.S. Supreme Court summarily affirmed.[44] The trial court had ordered that the woman be rehired, finding that "her overweight does not have deleterious effect upon her health or her ability to perform the job in question"; but neither the state appellate court nor the Supreme Court approved that test. Under the Constitution, therefore, a merely rational relationship between the weight ceiling and the job is probably sufficient.

May an applicant be rejected because of physical disabilities?

Most government agencies impose some requirements concerning physical and mental condition. Clearly, these requirements are valid in many occupations. For example, no one doubts that air traffic controllers should have good eyesight, or that telephone operators should have adequate hearing. But such obvious precepts do not cover all areas of public employment. Recently there have been many challenges to such restrictions, and the courts have begun to sort them out.

The most notable case was the Supreme Court decision in 1974 in *Cleveland Board of Education v. LaFleur*,[45] striking down mandatory maternity leave policies of school boards. Many school systems required pregnant teachers to take leave four or even five months before the scheduled date of delivery, and did not allow the teacher to return to work for a similar period after the birth. Such policies were usually justified on two grounds—keeping physically unfit teachers out of the classroom, and assuring continuity of instruction. The Supreme Court found that neither interest was rationally served by the maternity rules. The time requirements were in no direct way related to the teacher's physical condition or appearance. The "continuity" goal was actually undermined by the rule because the leave-taking time might fall within the middle of a marking period or even of a week. To the extent that valid state interests were involved, they could be served by less sweeping and more selective judgments about the capacity of individual pregnant teachers to continue in the classroom.

Since the *LaFleur* decision, there have been other challenges to physical disability–related public employment rules. A federal court of appeals has held that the Philadelphia public schools cannot bar all blind people from teaching sighted pupils.[46] The court relied in part on *LaFleur,* but recognized that that decision may have reflected a special and "fundamental" maternal interest in bearing children. Nonetheless, the exclusion of all blind teachers "creates an irrebuttable presumption in violation of the applicant's due process rights." The blind applicant was at least entitled to an individual determination of competence and suitability for the sighted classroom. The school board could not simply presume that all blind teachers were unqualified for regular teaching assignments.

This decision was, in fact, anticipated by an earlier (pre-*LaFleur*) New York decision to the same effect. A teacher in the public schools, with a good service record, had been involuntarily retired after becoming blind. In ordering that the teacher be given a hearing, the court posed the critical issue "not whether the teacher is blind but whether he is physically incapacitated from performing his duties as a teacher."[47] The court also suggested that some duties a blind teacher could not easily perform (grading papers, marking attendance roles, directing fire drills, and the like) should be assumed by sighted colleagues if necessary to effect the accommodation.

There is simply too little law on other kinds of physical disabilities to permit generalization. Several suits have been brought by epileptics to establish their eligibility for public employment, but no decisions on the merits have yet been reported. Presumably, much the same analysis as reflected in the blindness cases would be followed here, and some determination of individual competence for the particular position would be required.

A very recent federal case upheld the city of Detroit's practice of refusing employment as municipal bus drivers to people with a history of mental illness.[48] Since a physician reviewed the records in each case, no conclusive or irrebuttable presumption existed. Thus the court did not require an individual hearing or a psychiatric examination in every case, since an individual judgment (albeit cursory) was made of the medical records. If *LaFleur* were the sole guide on this issue, the Constitution might require a more elaborate procedure. But given the recent qualifications, the Detroit practice may satisfy the courts.

Thus far, we have spoken only of constitutional claims. The disabled worker, like the older worker, may receive greater protection from the legislature than from the courts. The Rehabilitation Act of 1973 protects both the mentally and physically handicapped against discrimination.[49] The law defines "handicapped individual" as one who (1) has a physical or mental impairment that substantially limits one or more of such person's major life activities, (2) had a record of such impairment, or (3) is regarded as having such an impairment.[50] It is not yet clear what impact these provisions will have on the rights of disabled persons seeking public employment. The Secretary of Health, Education and Welfare issued regulations in fall, 1976, to implement and enforce these statutory provisions.[51] The extent of remedies available under the law is not yet clear. In one early case, federal court in Texas has held that the Rehabilitation Act provisions do not provide a private remedy to handicapped persons alleging discrimination by federal contractors. The thrust of the law, said the court, was to provide protection to a class of persons, and to require employers to take steps to enhance that protection, but not to afford private redress.[52]

Meanwhile, comparable protection for the handicapped may develop under state and local law. (The New York court was influenced in the case of the blind teacher by a state statute providing that no person, otherwise qualified, should be denied employment as a teacher solely because of blindness or physical handicap, so long as the handicap did not interfere with the person's ability to perform the required duties.[53]) The laws of different states and cities vary considerably on the protection of the handicapped. Some fairly detailed knowledge of the local law is perhaps more necessary in this area than in the other areas considered in this chapter.

May a person be denied employment because of a criminal record?

The answer depends largely on the nature of the offense and, to a lesser degree, on the position sought. There is a spectrum of crimes from the most minor to the gravest, and the line of disqualification falls somewhere along it. The federal courts have suggested that a "traffic citation" could not be used as an employment bar, but that "a prior conviction of a serious offense would be a valid ground to disqualify a person from police work."[54] In federal cases, the courts have tended to uphold the Civil Service Commission's rejection of former criminals, whether the offense be shoplifting or manslaughter.[55] They have refused to demand any showing of a rational relationship between the offense and the position.

There have been some recent exceptions, however, from the federal district courts. Several cases involve isolated uses of marijuana, which (as one court recently put it) could not "possibly bear upon the applicant's fitness for employment as a Clerk II."[56] Even where marijuana use remains subject to criminal penalties, courts have been reluctant to extend the civil disabilities. Perhaps the boldest departure is *Butts v. Nichols*,[57] a 1974 federal court case holding unconstitutional an Iowa law that forbade the employment of ex-felons in the civil service. The court recognized that the state had legitimate interests in this area, but found those interests exceeded by the sweeping prohibition against hiring any felons. (Actually the ban was incomplete. Exceptions were made for certain high-level positions, to which the governmental interests would seem especially applicable. The irrationality of the statutory scheme was exaggerated by this negative correlation.) The line between felonies and misdemeanors has always been imprecise and somewhat archaic, and this was one of the problems. A person who had committed a misdemeanor bearing significantly on his civil reliability would be employable, while a merely technical felony would forever disqualify the offender. Thus the court concluded: "No consideration is given to the nature and seriousness of the crime in relation to the job sought. The time elapsing since the conviction, the degree of the felon's rehabilitation, and the circumstances under which the crime was committed are similarly ignored."[58] Finally, the court found the Iowa law invalid because it established a conclusive and irrebuttable presumption based solely on the commission of a single felony at some time in the past.

In later cases the courts have shown continued sympathy for the employment claims of persons charged with crime. A Louisiana appellate court has held that the arrest and incarceration of a civil service employee was not per se valid cause for dismissal.[59] A Kansas school teacher was held entitled to a new hearing following acquittal on marijuana charges for which he was originally dismissed.[60] And the California Supreme Court invalidated a state law barring an otherwise fit person from obtaining a teaching credential solely because the person had been convicted of a sex offense and had not received a "certificate of rehabilitation."[61]

One other recent case deserves mention. The New

York Transit Authority consistently denied employment to methadone users, most of whom were trying to break drug habits. A group of applicants (including one who had formerly been a highly competent transit employee) brought suit, challenging the constitutionality of the methadone bar. After an exhaustive analysis, the federal courts concluded that the policy violated both the due process and equal protection guarantees.[62] Some individual determination must be made of the suitability of particular applicants for particular positions; granting the Transit Authority's concern about hiring unstable motormen, there were many "non-operating" jobs to which such people could safely be assigned. Moreover, the side effects of methadone use (such as excessive constipation) were not in most cases disabling even for the more demanding or precarious operating positions. Finally, the Transit Authority to some extent gave away its own case since it usually conducted individual examinations of people with past mental illness, heart disease, or even tranquilizer use, rather than turning all such applicants away.

Here again, legislation may provide a measure of nonconstitutional protection. In the methadone case, the court noted a federal law providing that "no person may be denied or deprived of Federal civilian employment or a Federal professional or other license solely on the ground of prior drug abuse."[63] New York state and city both had similar policies. Some such laws are even more general, like the Florida statute providing that a person may not be denied government employment solely because of a prior felony conviction unless the offense "directly relates to the position of employment sought."[64] In the summer of 1977 the United States Department of labor issued a new rule making 97% of all parolees immediately eligible for unemployment benefits and for federally aided public works employment. The goal of this policy was to reduce the rate of repetition of crime by easing the path from prison to gainful employment and rehabilitation.[65] Such laws would go far toward reaching the result that the federal court reached on constitutional grounds in the Iowa case.

May a public employee or applicant object to the use of criminal records in determining eligibility?

The answer may vary with the nature of the position. One recent case suggests that investigation of the background of an applicant for police work might include a review of arrest records.[66] A person may, however, be able to limit the effect of an arrest record. Several courts have recently ordered particular kinds of arrest records to be destroyed,[67] and litigation is pending that would further restrict the dissemination of such records. Moreover, the Federal Bureau of Investigation has issued a procedure by which a person may obtain a copy of any records in its Identification Division (the central repository of such information), and may request of the agency submitting the record any changes that the person believes warranted.[68] The FBI will make changes requested by the initiating agency. Furter, in 1974, the FBI announced a new policy governing dissemination of its arrest records to banks and state and local agencies not involved in law enforcement. Such records will not be supplied if the arrest is more than a year old unless information concerning disposition is included in the request.[69] Finally, the legislatures of some states have required the expungement of arrest records derived from certain kinds of crimes, though this action usually takes the form of sealing the record rather than physically destroying it.[70] While the extent of protection varies from state to state, the public employee or applicant with an arrest record now has remedies that were not available even a few years ago, and current litigation may further enlarge these safeguards.

NOTES

1. *New York Times,* April 27, 1975, p. 63, col. 3.
2. *Heim v. McCall,* 239 U.S. 175 (1915).
3. *Sugarman v. Dougall,* 413 U.S. 634 (1973).
4. 413 U.S. at 634.
5. 413 U.S. at 647.
6. 413 U.S. at 649.
7. *Foley v. Connelie,* 419 F. Supp. 889 (S.D.N.Y. 1976) prob. juris noted, 430 U.S. 944 (1977).
8. *Norwick v. Nyquist,* 417 F. Supp. 913 (S.D.N.Y. 1976).
9. *Chavez-Salido v. Cabell,* 427 F. Supp. 158 (C.D. Cal. 1977).
10. *New York Times,* June 8, 1977, p. 60, col. 3-4.
11. *Nyquist v. Mauclet,* 432 U.S. — (1977).
12. 426 U.S. 88 (1976).
13. *Mow Sun Wong v. Hampton,* 435 F. Supp. 37 (N.D. Cal. 1977).
14. *De Canas v. Bica,* 424 U.S. 351 (1976).
15. *Saxbe v. Bustos,* 419 U.S. 65 (1974).
16. *Graham v. Richardson,* 403 U.S. 365, 376 (1971).
17. *C.D.R. Enterprises, Ltd. v. Board of Education,* 412 F. Supp. 1164 (S.D.N.Y. 1976).
18. *Lefkowitz v. C.D.R. Enterprises,* 429 U.S. 1031 (1977).
19. *McCarthy v. Philadelphia Civil Service Commission,* 424 U.S. 645 (1976). See also *Detroit Police Officers Association v. City of Detroit,* 385 Mich. 519, 190 N.W.2d 97 (1971), appeal dismissed, 405 U.S. 950 (1971).
20. *Shapiro v. Thompson,* 394 U.S. 618 (1969).
21. *Wardwell v. Board of Education,* 529 F.2d 625 (6th Cir. 1976); see also *Pittsburgh Federation of Teachers v. Aaron,* 417 F. Supp. 94 (W.D. Pa. 1976); cf. *Mogle v. Sevier County School District,* 540 F.2d 478 (10th Cir. 1976).
22. *Town of Milton v. Civil Service Commission,* 365 Mass. 368, 312 N.E.2d 188 (1974); *People ex rel. Holland v. Bligh Construction Co.,* 61 Ill. 2d 258, 335 N.E.2d 469 (1975).
23. *McIlvaine v. Pennsylvania,* 454 Pa. 129, 309 A.2d 801 (1973), appeal dismissed, 415 U.S. 986 (1974); *Weisbrod v. Lynn,* 420 U.S. 940 (1975).
24. *Murgia v. Massachusetts Board of Retirement,* 376 F. Supp. 753 (D. Mass. 1974).
25. *Massachusetts Board of Retirement v. Murgia,* 427 U.S. 307 (1976).
26. 427 U.S. at 313.

27. *Shapiro v. Thompson*, 394 U.S. 618 (1969).
28. See *Usery v. Tamiami Trail Tours, Inc.*, 531 F.2d 224 (5th Cir. 1976). But cf. *Rodriguez v. Taylor*, No. CA 75-1738 (E.D. Pa. 1976), reported in 10 *Clearinghouse Review* 459 (1976).
29. 29 U.S.C. § 623 (a) (1970).
30. 29 U.S.C. § 623(f) (1970).
31. *Usery v. Tamiami Trail Tours, Inc.*, 531 F.2d 224 (5th Cir. 1976).
32. 29 U.S.C. §623 (f) (2) (1940).
33. *United Air Lines, Inc. v. McMann*, 46 U.S. Law Week 4043 (1977).
34. *Aaron v. Davis*, 414 F. Supp. 453 (E.D. Ark. 1976).
35. *Rogers v. Exxon, Inc.*, 45 550 f. 2d 834 (3d Cir. 1977).
36. *Bertrand v. Orkin Exterminating Co.*, 419 f. Supp. 1123 (N.D. Ill. 1977).
37. *New York Times*, See 46 U.S. Law Week 2198 (1977); N.Y. Times, Oct. 24, 1977, p. 19, col. 1; July 11, 1977, p. 40, col. 3; Sept. 24, 1977, p. 1, col. 6.
38. *New Jersey State Police Benevolent Association v. Town of Morristown*, 65 N.J. 160, 320 A.2d 465 (1974).
39. *Dothard v. Rawlinson*, 432 U.S. — (1977).
40. See *Fox v. Washington*, F. Supp. (D.D.C. 1975).
41. *New York Times*, June 4, 1975, p. 59, col. 4.
42. *Blodgett v. Board of Trustees*, 1 Civ. No. 27647 (Cal. Ct. App. September 23, 1971).
43. *Parolisi v. Board of Examiners*, 55 Misc. 2d 546, 285 N.Y.S.2d 936 (1967).
44. *Metropolitan Dade County v. Wolf*, 274 So. 2d 584 (Fla. Dist. Ct. App. 1973), *cert. denied*, 414 U.S. 1116 (1974).
45. 414 U.S. 632 (1974).
46. *Gurmankin v. Costanzo*, 411 F. Supp. 982 (E.D. Pa. 1976), affirmed, 556 F.2d 184 (3d Cir. 1977).
47. *Bevan v. New York State Teachers Retirement System*, 74 Misc. 2d 443, 345 N.Y.S. 2d 921 (1973).
48. *Spencer v. Toussaint*, 408 F. Supp. 1067 (E.D. Mich. 1976).
49. 29 U.S.C. § 794 (1970).
50. 29 U.S.C. § 701(6) (1970).
51. 41 Fed. Reg. 29548 (1976).
52. *Rogers v. Frito-Lay, Inc.*, 46 U.S. Law Week 2007 (N.D. Tex. 1977).
53. New York Education Law § 3004.
54. *United States v. City of Chicago*, 411 F. Supp. 218, 235 (N.D. Ill. 1976).
55. *Gueroy v. Hampton*, 510 F. 2d 1222 (D.C. Cir. 1974); *Taffel v. Hampton*, 463 F.2d 251 (5th Cir. 1972).
56. *Osterman v. Paulk*, 387 F. Supp. 669 (S.D. Fla. 1974); cf.

O'Shea v. Blatchford, 346 F. Supp. 742 (S.D.N.Y. 1972). But cf. *Young v. Hampton*, 420 F. Supp. 1358 (S.D. Ill. 1976).

57. 381 F. Supp. 573 (S.D. Iowa 1974).
58. 381 F. Supp. at 581.
59. *Brown v. Louisiana Health & Human Resources Administration*, No. 11,179 (La. Ct. App. June 13, 1977), 11 Clearinghouse Review 382 (1977).
60. *Bogart v. Unified School District*, 423 F. Supp. 895 (D. Kan. 1977).
61. *Newland v. Board of Governors of California Community Colleges*, 567 P.2d 254 (Cal. 1977).
62. *Bezar v. New York City Transit Authority*, 399 F. Supp. 1032 (S.D.N.Y. 1975), affirmed, 558 F.2d 97 (2d Cir. 1976).
63. 21 U.S.C. § 1180(c) (1970).
64. Fla. Stat. § 112.011.
65. *New York Times*, June 13, 1977, p. 18, col. 6.
66. *United States v. City of Chicago*, 411 F. Supp. 218, 235 (N.D. Ill. 1976).
67. *Sullivan v. Murphy*, 478 F.2d 938 (D.C. Cir. 1973); *Menard v. Saxbe*, 498 F.2d 1017 (D.C. Cir. 1974).
68. *The Privacy Report*, Vol. II, No. 8, June 1975, p. 8.
69. If you wish such information, send your name, date and place of birth, a set of fingerprints, and $5 to: FBI, Identification Division, Washington, D.C. 20537.
70. *Massachusetts General Laws*, Chap. 276, Sec. 100A (Supp. 1977).

III

Public Employment and Freedom
of Speech

Louisiana governor Huey Long discharged the editor of the state university's daily newspaper after reading an editorial attack on his administration. "I ain't payin' nobody to criticize me," Long was quoted in justification. The history of public employment is full of examples of reprisals against allegedly disloyal, hostile, critical or even ungrateful government workers. Usually the reasons given for such actions, if any, are softer than Huey Long's characteristically blunt statement, but the rationale may be equally simple.

A recent *cause célèbre* of this sort involved one of the early victims of the Watergate era. A. Ernest Fitzgerald was a cost accountant in the Pentagon, assigned to review the production of the contract for the C-5A transport. Fitzgerald discovered that the contractor had experienced a cost overrun of some $2 million, and he so reported to a congressional committee. Fitzgerald was soon dismissed from his position. The reason given at the time was "economy." Later, when Fitzgerald sought review through the Civil Service system, the real reason came to light: Fitzgerald had become a target of the Nixon administration, which hoped to silence his criticism by removing him from office. A memorandum from Alexander Butterfield (the White House aide who later revealed the existence of the taping system) to H. R. Haldeman advised that the administration "should let him [Fitzgerald] bleed" because "he must be given very low marks in loyalty; and after all, loyalty is the name of the game." After six years of fighting, Fitzgerald finally regained his federal employment, with back pay, and recouped his court costs and other expenses.[1] Others who have "blown the whistle" on government irregularities have been either less fortunate or less persistent.

This chapter concerns critics, whistle blowers, and other government employees whose controversial speech or writing or suspected disloyalty gets them into trouble. We begin with the matter of loyalty oaths and other security tests.

May a public employee be required to take an oath of office?

Yes. The Supreme Court has held that the traditional oath of allegiance, long required of persons holding many public positions (including the presidency of the United States) is constitutional.[2] The particular case involved a Massachusetts law requiring office holders to swear (or affirm) that "I will uphold and defend the Constitution and laws of the United States of America and the Constitution of the Commonwealth of Massachusetts and that I will oppose the overthrow of the government of the United States of America or of this Commonwealth by force, violence, or by any illegal or unconstitutional method."[3] In sustaining this language, the Court stressed the historic role of such oaths of allegiance, even though the formulation might vary between states. In an earlier case, the Court had noted that "the oath of constitutional support requires an individual assuming public responsibilities to affirm

. . . that he will endeavor to perform his public duties lawfully."[4]

May an oath concerning political belief be required?

In general, no oath broader than the oath of allegiance may be required of an applicant for public employment. The Supreme Court has struck down many different oaths, either because they were too vague and uncertain or because they asked the applicant to surrender constitutional rights of expression or belief. Such oaths have been both positive and negative in nature. Of the positive types, the Court in 1964 invalidated a Washington requirement that state employees "will by precept and example promote respect for the flag and [federal and state] institutions, reverence for law and order and undivided allegiance to the . . . government."[5] The basis for the decision was the vagueness and breadth of the required commitment: "The teacher who refused to salute the flag or advocated refusal might well be accused of breaching his promise." Since that decision, there have been few attempts to require public employees to take positive oaths broader than the traditional oath of allegiance.

More troublesome have been oaths calling for a renunciation or disclaimer of beliefs and affiliations. Another part of the Washington requirement demanded that every applicant disavow being a "subversive person" or a member of a "subversive organization"—language that the Court also found unconstitutionally vague.[6] Several years later, the Court made even clearer its objection to forcing a person to forswear membership in suspect groups. In striking down an Arizona law that barred from public employment anyone who would not disclaim membership in the Communist Party or any other organization dedicated to the overthrow of the government, the Court explained: "Those who join an organization but do not share its unlawful activities surely pose no threat, either as citizens or as public employees."[7]

Such a law, continued the Court, infringes on protected freedoms of expression and association, and "rests on the doctrine of 'guilt by association,' which has no place here."

May an applicant be required to disavow membership in a specific organization?

Not unless the disclaimer is confined to (1) active membership, (2) membership with knowledge of the organization's illegal aims, and (3) membership with the specific intent of furthering those aims. Ordinary membership, or even active membership in an organization that has unlawful aims, may not be proscribed. Thus a person who joins the Communist Party to promote civil rights, or to discuss economic theory, may not be denied public employment even though such a person holds office or has some other active role in the party.

Recent litigation has successfully challenged loyalty-type questions put to applicants for federal employment. People seeking positions in the Veterans Administration had been required to indicate whether or not they belonged to the Communist Party or any subdivision of the party. They also had to tell whether at the time of application, or at any time within the past ten years, they had belonged to any group that, to their knowledge, advocated the violent overthrow of the United States or any state or local government. If an applicant responded affirmatively to the second question, he was then asked whether membership involved the specific intent to further the unlawful aims of the organization. If that question was answered affirmatively, the applicant had to list the names of any such organizations and the dates of membership. These questions were challenged on constitutional grounds by several potential VA applicants who wished to avoid the inquiries.

The court held that the questionnaire impermissibly intruded upon the applicant's First Amendment freedoms.[8] Although government clearly has the power to keep out of public employment people actively engaged in promoting its violent overthrow, that objective must be served through sensitive means. On the basis of Supreme Court decisions dealing with admission to the bar and other government benefits,[9] the Court held the VA questions defective for two reasons—first, because the procedure for handling affirmative answers (and thus for avoiding an automatic disqualification) was deficient; second, an applicant could be disqualified for knowing, active membership in an organization that merely taught or discussed the overthrow of the government but did not incite persons to revolution or disruption. In short, the questionnaire failed to distinguish between mere advocacy and incitement (the former is constitutionally protected; the latter may be reached by narrow constraints).

Several months later, in fall 1976, the U.S. Civil Service Commission agreed to drop all political loyalty questions from the standard application forms for federal positions.[10] This action came after other federal district courts had reached the same decision as that in the VA case, and no court had sustained the questions. Thus the issue of whether government may ask applicants about membership in political organizations may now be essentially moot, although there is no guarantee that similar inquiries will not be reinstated in the future.

What is the federal loyalty-security apparatus (other than membership questions), and how does it work?

Although major reliance has been placed on oaths and inquiries as a means of excluding subversive persons from public employment, other barriers still exist. Federal law provides for the suspension of employees in the interests of national security,[11] although even as far back as 1956 the Supreme Court limited the scope of this procedure to relatively sensitive positions that could significantly affect national interests.[12] Federal law once barred from employment in a defense facility any person belonging to an organization designated by the Subversive Activities Control Board as a Communist-action group, but in 1967 the Supreme Court held this proscription unconstitutional. In *United States v. Robel,*[13] the Court found that such a law imposed guilt by association, and forced a person to choose between livelihood and a degree of membership protected by general First Amendment rights of citizenship. After several more skirmishes, the listing of organizations as "Communist-action" or "Communist-front" was abolished in the summer of 1974, and may no longer be used for any purpose. This step also virtually eliminated any significant role for the once ominous and powerful Subversive Activities Control Board.

What remains is the procedure for loyalty checks on people being considered for or actually appointed to sensitive federal positions. The scope of the investigation depends on the sensitivity of the position, but will typically include at least a fingerprint check with the FBI (which will now reveal virtually any arrest as well as conviction records—though see *infra,* Chapter III) and inquiries to other law enforcement agencies, former employers, landlords, and perhaps other references. If evidence impugning the applicant's or employee's loyalty emerges during such an investigation, the agency may suspend the employee or even remove such a person by following the statutorily prescribed procedures[14] (see Chapter VII). Probationary (i.e., nonpermanent) employees, who would be most commonly subject to the results of a security check, enjoy only the rather limited right to submit written statements to refute such charges and may not under the general federal Civil Service law demand a hearing.[15] There is one important qualification: If the agency has established a more rigorous procedure for dealing with security matters, it may not bypass or shortcut that procedure in a particular case; the Supreme Court has held specifically in this context that a government agency is bound to follow its own rules even though it may not have been legally required to adopt them in the first place.[16]

The range of information that may be considered in determining whether an applicant or employee poses any risk to the national security is quite broad. It may include law violations, drunkenness or drug addiction, mental illness, sexual deviation, and other conditions;[17] in Chapter V, we will consider more extensively the degree to which a person's private life or behavior may disqualify him or her from public employment.

Finally, there are provisions restricting the reemployment of a person who is dismissed or denied employment for security reasons. Such a person may be rehired in the same or a different department only if the head of the department finds that such employment is clearly consistent with the interests of national security. In addition, the appointment of such a person to a different agency or department may be made only after the head of the new agency consults the Civil Service Commission, which may determine whether the person is eligible for employment in a department other than the original one.[18]

Are nonpolitical associations also protected by the Constitution?

Yes. Although most suspect associations are political, the public employee's freedom of association is not limited to such groups. Several years ago, the Baltimore Police Department rejected an applicant who revealed that he belonged to a nudist society. There was no indication that the applicant would refuse to wear clothes on the job or to enforce laws against indecent exposure. Nor was there any evidence of illegal activity on the part of the nudist group. Thus the federal court held that the applicant's First Amendment freedoms include "the right to associate with any person of one's choosing for the purpose of advocating and promoting legitimate, albeit controversial, political, social and economic views."[19] The police commissioner had failed to demonstrate any governmental interest that out-weighed the strong associational interest of the appli-cant. While such cases are rare outside the political context, the basic precepts apply equally to other forms of association.

Is the language of an oath significant?

Yes. Many of the earlier Supreme Court cases turned on the vagueness and uncertainty of language, such as that of the Florida oath, which required em-ployees to swear that they would not "lend aid, sup-port, advise, counsel or influence to the Communist Party."[20] Later cases have also stressed the need for precision and clarity especially because the exercise of First Amendment liberties might be "chilled" or dis-couraged by unclear or imprecise language.[21]

On the other hand, there may be such a thing as ex-cessive precision. If a law is directed at a specific, named organization, and if it carries criminal penalties, it might violate another constitutional provision. A de-cade ago, the Supreme Court struck down an act of Congress that made it a crime for any officer of the Communist Party to serve as an officer of a labor union. While the government may have reason to pro-tect unions from Communist influence, that goal could not be served by singling out a designated group of people. This was what the framers of the Constitution had in mind by forbidding "bills of attainder."[22] (A bill of attainder is a law passed after the fact making cer-tain prior conduct criminal, or imposing penalties with-out notice at the time of the action.) Thus an oath focused *too* narrowly upon a particular named group or organization might be struck down for reasons quite different from those that involve loose and vague lan-guage.

May an applicant be required to forswear future po-litical activity or affiliation?

Constitutional protection for past or present political

association applies with even greater force to the future. It is one thing to ask an applicant about groups to which he or she has belonged or now belongs; it is another and more hazardous matter to ask a person to agree for the indefinite future to steer clear of groups that may not even exist and can at best be loosely described. Even in theory, the most that an applicant could be forced to forswear is knowing, active membership in illegal organizations with a specific intent to further those illegal aims. As a practical matter, it seems unlikely that a rational government agency would design such an oath even if it would pass constitutional muster.

This discussion should not leave the impression that government agencies have no proper concern with security. The courts have, on the contrary, acknowledged this interest in every case involving loyalty and security issues.[23] But courts have insisted that subversion must be curbed by means that are narrower and more precise than loyalty oaths; indeed, there is reason to believe that people truly bent on sabotage would have few qualms about signing such an oath, while a person of impeccable loyalty but strong conscience might be troubled and would thus forfeit the job for reasons unrelated to any governmental interest. In this way loyalty oaths may actually have been counterproductive, and not simply ineffective or offensive.

May an applicant be asked to list organizations to which he or she belongs?

The answer depends very much on the scope and purpose of the inquiry. Some years ago, the Supreme Court held that Arkansas could not require all teachers to list every year all the organizations to which they belonged. Such a demand, said the Court, went "far beyond what might be justified in the exercise of the State's legitimate inquiry into the fitness and competency of its teachers" and threatened to deter teachers from perfectly lawful associations.[24] The Court hinted that *some* teachers might be asked at *some* times about *some* associations, but it has had no occasion to define the scope of permissible inquiry in this sensitive area. There may be a difference between requests for information from an initial applicant for public employment and from an incumbent during the term of employment; the Arkansas case was concerned only with the rights of people already employed in the state school system.

The type of organization may also be relevant. It seems doubtful that government has a valid interest in asking about memberships that would not jeopardize a person's eligibility for employment—that is, groups in which even knowing, active membership would not be disqualifying. Presumably, government has a valid interest only in knowing whether an applicant belongs to an organization that could be outlawed, since other affiliations are protected by the Constitution.

May a belief in God be required of public employees?

No. The precise question has not been decided, but there are related cases. Most pertinent is a Supreme Court decision that Maryland could not require a person applying for a notary public's commission to express or affirm a belief in God. Under the religious guarantees of the First Amendment to the Constitution, the Court held that government may not "pass laws or impose requirements which aid all religions as against nonbelievers, and neither can it aid those religions based on a belief in the existence of God as against those religions founded on different beliefs."[25] It would seem to follow that an applicant for employment may not be required to swear a belief in God—much less allegiance to a particular faith. Nor may a person be barred from government employment because of a particular religious affiliation; a federal district court has recently held that Maryland could not constitutionally bar clergymen from serving in the state legislature.[26] A case now pending before the Supreme Court questions Tennessee's law—apparently the only one in the country—which bars clergymen from holding any public office, including membership in the legislature.[27]

There has been considerable recent litigation on the employment of persons with special religious calendars. The Supreme Court held in the summer of 1977 that a private employer was required only to make reasonable accommodations to the special needs of persons who worship on Saturday and was not required to disrupt the regular work schedule.[28] Lower federal courts have reached similar conclusions in public employment—one in a case involving a Sabbatarian Worker in a small post office,[29] and the other in the case of a fireman whose Saturday worship preference could not reasonably be accommodated.[30] Yet the agency must show that efforts have been made to reconcile its scheduling needs and the employee's religious practice.

Is a public employee free to protest or criticize government or agency policy?

In general, public employees retain their First Amendment freedom of expression when they enter public service. But there are important exceptions and qualifications, which require some elaboration here. Important interests must be weighed on both sides of the balance. Not only do the interests of the individual employee favor freedom of expression; in addition, society at large benefits by allowing government workers to speak candidly about agency practices and policies. On the other hand, important interests of government may militate against complete freedom. The efficiency, morale, and discipline of the public service, it is argued, may be impaired by excessive controversy and criticism. The appearance of neutrality, which is essential to public service, could be jeopardized if workers give excessive public vent to differences of opinion. The public image of an agency, citizen confidence in its work, and ultimately its capacity to obtain legislative support and funding might also be adversely affected by outspoken staff members. Finally, public employees often possess highly sensitive information, the untimely disclosure of which could seriously damage governmental interests or even endanger lives. For all these reasons, some limitations on expression in the public sector have been upheld.

The starting point is the 1968 Supreme Court decision in *Pickering v. Board of Education.*[31] The Court held that a teacher could not be dismissed for statements about school board policy without "proof of false statements knowingly and recklessly made." Public charges containing minor errors were within the public employee's constitutional freedom of expression. But the Court noted many factors that the *Pickering* case did not involve and that might alter the outcome—personal attacks on immediate superiors, revelations of confidential information, disruptive consequences, etc. The statements of the teacher in this case fell clearly within the scope of the newly declared constitutional standard.

The *Pickering* case left open many issues that have been the subject of later decisions, and that we will examine in the ensuing sections.

For what stated reason may a critic be disciplined?

Seldom do government regulations contain a specific prohibition against making statements critical of agency policy or anything of that sort. Typically, the reprisals against critics are based on very general language that fails to give adequate warning of the consequences. In the federal civil service, the relevant language permits removal or suspension "only for such cause as will promote the efficiency of the service."[32] Courts have been rather deferential to the Civil Service Commission in their interpretation of this very broad language. At the state and local level, the basis for dismissal is also imprecise—a Nevada school teacher was dismissed for "unprofessional conduct" because he publicly opposed compulsory school attendance laws;[33] and a Connecticut teacher was dismissed for "misconduct" after she distributed leaflets attacking the school administration and its policies.[34] These and other recent cases have upheld the use of such vague statutory language as the basis for dismissing critics of government policies.

Does the nature of the issue affect the scope of criticism or protest?

The *Pickering* case spoke of issues of "public importance" as the basis for the privilege of criticism. Presumably, mere gossip would not come within this term, although many facets of the private life of a public official may be proper subjects of public comment and interest. Even a protest about working conditions within a government agency may raise issues of "public importance" unless it reflects purely personal pique. Presumably, courts would take a rather tolerant view of the scope of commentary for these purposes, and would consider a matter to be of "public importance" unless the contrary were clearly shown.

Does the nature of the agency affect the scope of criticism?

Yes. The need for internal discipline and the potential effect of public criticism will vary considerably among agencies. For example, a federal court of appeals has held that a tense situation in the Panama Canal Zone limited the rights of members of the police force to criticize agency policies.[35] Yet police officers are not deprived of free speech simply because of the "paramilitary" nature of police agencies, as other cases indicate. The Maryland Court of Appeals sustained the right of a Baltimore policeman to make highly critical statements about agency morale on a local television station, even though the consequences for the agency could be quite harmful.[36] Another federal appellate court has upheld the right of a controversial Chicago policeman to protest publicly the policies of his superiors.[37] Similar decisions have been reached with regard to outspoken firemen, further indicating that the need for internal discipline is merely one relevant factor.[38]

Is the status of the employee relevant to the scope of criticism?

Yes. The relationship between the critic and the subject of criticism is clearly pertinent. In the *Pickering* case, the Supreme Court recognized a strong government interest in regulating statements "directed toward any person with whom [the critic] would normally be in contact in the course of his daily work" and stressed the risks of jeopardizing "harmony among co-workers."[39] The *Pickering* court also noted that "positions in public employment in which the relationship between superior and subordinate is of such a personal and intimate nature that certain forms of public criticism of the superior by the subordinate would seriously undermine the effectiveness of the working relationship between them can also be imagined." Several recent cases have stressed the effect of critical speech on close personal and professional relationships, and have upheld dismissals accordingly. A school superintendent was discharged for denouncing publicly school board members seeking reelection, and a first assistant district attorney was fired for statements so critical of his superior's handling of cases that the working relationship between the two men was seriously impaired. Both dismissals were upheld by federal courts of appeals, recognizing the exception derived from *Pickering*.[40]

The relationship of the critic to the source of the information is also pertinent. The Court suggested in *Pickering* that the result might have been different if "a teacher has carelessly made false statements about matters so closely related to the day-to-day operations of the schools and any harmful impact on the public would be difficult to counter because of the teacher's presumed greater access to the real facts."[41] One might thus infer that the closer one gets to the source, the narrower is the latitude for expression. On the other hand, the privilege might expand with the degree of expertise. A dissenting judge in the state court in *Pickering* observed that "teachers are in closer contact with the actual operation of the schools than anyone else and the public should not be deprived of their views."[42] The Maryland court in the Baltimore policeman's case stressed the importance of allowing the officer "to speak freely on matters of public importance, particularly matters to which he had experienced expertise."[43] Other cases have suggested that the greater the knowledge of the speaker, the broader the freedom that should be allowed—even though it is true that the agency may find it more difficult to respond to an expert critic.

Sometimes the criticism concerns a matter on which the speaker has no special expertise. In the late 1960s, a Peace Corps Volunteer in Chile wrote a letter to a local newspaper that was critical of American foreign policy in Southeast Asia—a matter that was neither within his special competence nor his job responsibility. He was dismissed for violating a Peace Corps directive against making such statements abroad. Despite the lack of any logical connection between the public position and the subject of comment, the court found that the volunteer's First Amendment rights had been violated.[44] On the other hand, a federal court of appeals around the same time upheld the dismissal of a teacher of Vietnamese military personnel who had strayed from his text to comment critically on American foreign policy.[45] In addition to the attenuated relationship between the assigned topic and the teacher's remarks, the court stressed the potentially harmful effect upon international relations in a particularly sensitive period.

Is the tone of the criticism relevant?

Clearly so. In cases in which critics have been reinstated, the courts have sometimes remarked upon the restrained or responsible tone of the criticism. In the

Canal Zone police case, which involved a poem and a letter, by contrast, the court found that the objectionable poem was an "intemperate lampoon" and that the letter had a "contemptuous quality."[46] A Connecticut case sustained the dismissal of a teacher partly because of the tone and language of the charges made against a superior, whom the teacher publicly denounced as a liar.[47] Yet the courts have made clear that criticism need not be mild or gentle in order to merit constitutional protection under the *Pickering* doctrine; otherwise, warned a New York court, "those who criticize in any area where criticism is permissible would either be discouraged from exercising their right or would do so in such innocuous terms as would make the criticism seem ineffective or obsequious."[48] There are numerous recent examples of cases in which the use of strong language has been sustained, and quite properly so under the First Amendment, even though the tone of the statement undoubtedly affects the legal issue.[49]

The status of profanity and taboo words is at least as complex. In several cases, teachers have been dismissed, and their dismissals upheld by the courts, for using allegedly obscene or taboo materials in the classroom. While the outcome may vary with the nature of the material, its relevance to the subject matter, and the age level of the students, even high school English teachers have not always fared well in this sensitive area.[50] Yet at least one court has recognized the risks of discharging a public employee for the use of taboo language, however offensive it may be to many listeners:

That the use of one word in lieu of another may conform more closely to the canons of good taste does not justify severe sanctions against those who use the offending word. To prohibit particular words substantially increases the risk that ideas will also be suppressed in the process.[51]

What significance do the form and format of the criticism have?

Most of the "protest" cases have involved either written letters or public speeches critical of agency policy. The fact that a speech may be broadcast over radio or television may (as in the case of the Baltimore policeman) intensify its probable impact but certainly does not reduce the scope of protected expression. If the criticism receives little or no attention as a result of the medium chosen for its dissemination, the low probability of harm may help the employee's cause.

Intriguing problems are posed by more novel forms of protest. A probation officer was discharged for filing a lawsuit seeking the integration of Alabama child care institutions. This action violated a juvenile court judge's order prohibiting staff members from filing suits affecting the operation of his court. The federal court of appeals first held that the probation officer had been unconstitutionally discharged, since there was no evidence of probable disruption as a result of his court suit—"the discharge of the probation officer was based on nothing more than the judge's subjective apprehensions of disturbance to the court and, as such, was unwarranted and in violation of the employee's First Amendment freedoms."[52] Later, the full court of appeals overruled this judgment, however, because of the very special relationship involved.[53]

There have also been recent cases involving "symbolic protest" in various nonverbal forms. Black employees of the Census Bureau protested alleged racial discrimination in hiring and promotion by picketing the lunch room, and eventually surrounding the table where two supervisors were eating.[54] Staff members of the Library of Congress staged a sit-in demonstration in the reading room of the Library, protesting alleged racial discrimination.[55] In both cases, the courts sustained the dismissals because of the disruptive nature of the conduct. Also sustained by the federal courts was the dismissal of a San Francisco probations officer who displayed on the wall of his office a poster praising Angela Davis and two other fugitives from justice. The court found the poster inimical to the employee's assigned role as a counselor and advisor, and potentially threatening to harmony within a racially mixed agency.[56]

Not all symbolic protest has fared so badly. Two teachers in upstate New York won their cases in the federal courts—one having been dismissed for wearing a black armband in protest against the Vietnam war,[57] the other for refusing as a matter of conscience to lead the salute of the flag and the pledge of allegiance.[58] In both cases, the court stressed that the students involved were mature and could form independent judgments on controversial issues. Had the incidents involved elementary school teachers, the outcome might have been different.

It is hard to generalize about the relationship between the format of protest and the scope of constitutional protection. Most cases involve conventional expression through the spoken or written word. Most of the principles affecting the public employee's right to criticize have evolved in this context. Increasingly, however, protest is expressed in less traditional forms—lawsuits, sit-ins, and the display of posters, buttons, armbands, and the like. Courts have adapted to these new forms of expression in other contexts and presumably will do so in the realm of public employment as well.

Must actual harm to the agency be shown in order to support dismissal of a critic?

No. What is critical is the risk or probability of harm and not the actual effect. A seemingly innocuous statement may, for reasons beyond the speaker's intent and control, be highly damaging. On the other hand, the maker of a highly inflammatory statement may not take refuge in the fact that disaster is in fact averted. It is the probability, not the actuality, that counts.

Is the amount of time devoted to criticism relevant?

Yes. If criticizing one's own agency takes away time supposed to be spent performing assigned duties, an employee may be discharged for reasons unrelated to the content of the criticism. In most cases, the time involved has been minimal, and the protesting has been done on evenings, weekends, or lunch hours. In several cases where critics have lost in the courts, though, the diversion of time and attention from the job may have been a factor—the Census Bureau and Library of Congress protests, the probations officer's poster, the making of antiwar remarks to Vietnamese personnel in a class on a wholly different subject. One possible solution to this conflict, of course, is taking a leave of absence for the time committed to critical activity. Such leaves may not always be granted, however, and if taken without permission may get the employee into serious trouble. Witness the case of the University of North Carolina faculty member who canceled a class in order to participate in an antiwar moratorium, and whose appointment was not renewed in part as a result of this absence. Even though the activity itself was protected by the First Amendment, the Court sustained the nonrenewal for violation of a university policy that in effect required regular faculty attendance at classes. "That the failure to carry out this responsibility," said the court, "was because he was elsewhere exercising his right of free expression does not excuse his unwillingness to perform those duties which he had undertaken."[59]

May an employee be required to "clear" a critical statement through agency channels?

In the *Pickering* case, the Supreme Court left open the question of "how far teachers can be required by narrowly drawn grievance procedures to submit complaints about the operation of the schools to their superiors for action thereon before bringing the complaints before the public."[60] A number of courts have struck down such "clearance" procedures. In the Panama Canal Zone police case, the procedure was voided because it was excessively vague and because it had not been applied consistently.[61] An Iowa court struck down a clearance procedure as applied to firemen, even though this was a "semi-military organization," because there had been no showing of "an impairment of the public service."[62] A civilian employee in a U.S. Naval Shipyard bypassed the grievance procedure in sending his complaint directly to the Secretary of the Navy, and was upheld for doing so.[63]

Probably the most celebrated case of clearance requirements came out the other way. Victor Marchetti, a former agent of the Central Intelligence Agency, wrote a book about CIA activities. The agency went to court to obtain an injunction against the publication of certain allegedly classified materials in the manuscript. The district court issued the injunction, and the decision was upheld on appeal.[64] The Supreme Court declined to review the case. The lower courts ruled that Marchetti had waived his right to publish freely when he signed the CIA secrecy agreement. To this extent, the courts upheld the clearance procedure—although the case may be unusual both because of the specific agreement that a CIA employee signs, and because of the highly sensitive nature of the material presumably subject to review.

Despite the trend of the cases, a public employee would be unwise to bypass an internal grievance procedure or clearance requirement. As a practical matter, complaints may sometimes be solvable within the agency without the risk of external appeals. Under the *Pickering* case, a precise and open clearance procedure might be binding, at least if it were responsive to the complaint.

What protection exists for public employees who "blow the whistle" on agency errors, omissions, graft, corruption, etc.?

As mentioned at the beginning of this chapter, perhaps the most celebrated recent case of a "whistle blower" is that of A. Ernest Fitzgerald, the civilian employee of the Pentagon who testified to Congress about serious cost overruns in the building of a military transport plane. Federal officials, highly displeased by the embarrassing disclosure, dismissed Fitzgerald. After four years of internal appeals, Fitzgerald succeeded in regaining federal employment; a Civil Service appeals examiner found that his dismissal had been improperly predicated on his "whistle blowing," rather than on an alleged economy drive. Fitzgerald's case had cost several hundred thousand dollars in legal fees and other expenses. So he went to court to recover these costs, and won a substantial judgment, which, in the words of the *New York Times,* "set a precedent for all government workers who feel they have been wrongfully dismissed from their jobs."[65]

Other "whistle blowers" have met with varying success. Courts have generally been sympathetic to the claims of such persons that they could seek effective redress only outside the agency, and have weighed carefully the strong public interest in full disclosure of agency wrongdoing. In the post-Watergate era, it seems likely that such revelations will receive even greater protection. (Indeed, legislation introduced in Congress, but not yet adopted, would protect from reprisal most federal employees who, like Fitzgerald, make public information that is critical or damaging to the agency by which they are employed.[66])

Two recent developments at the federal level may complicate the issue. In June, 1977, Alan K. Campbell, the new chairman of the United States Civil Service Commission, announced a new commitment of the Carter administration to protect dissent within the Federal Service. Campbell declared that "dissent certainly is possible within the public service, and should be encouraged; it should be pointed to trying to improve the quality of service the government is providing."[67] Action has not yet been taken, however, to implement that commitment, and its extent therefore remains unclear.

Several months earlier the Supreme Court held that a teacher who had been dismissed following public criticism of school board policy was not automatically entitled to reinstatement. But the Justices did direct the lower court to hold a further hearing, since the school board had not shown it would have reached the same result without considering the teacher's protected speech. If the board could make such a showing, then the dismissal would apparently stand even though it may have been motivated in part by expression of the kind *Pickering* protects.[68]

When does the First Amendment right to petition for redress of grievances protect a public employee?

The First Amendment protects the "right to petition the Government for redress of grievances" along with the freedoms of speech, press, assembly, and worship. For federal employees, the right of petition has also received statutory protection through a law that provides that "the right of employees, individually or collectively, to petition Congress or a member of Congress, or to furnish information to either House of Congress, or to a committee or member thereof, may not be interfered with or denied."[69] The courts have recognized that such petitions must be allowed, even when they are annoying to Congress.[70] If, however, a critical communication is sent outside the channels of governmental grievances, it may lose its character (and thus its special sanctity) as a petition. This is not to say that its sender is for that reason alone subject to dismissal, but only that his fate must be decided by the more general standards outlined elsewhere in this chapter and not by the special safeguards available to intragovernmental petitioners.

What standards govern the nonprotest speech of public employees?

Virtually all the cases in which public employees have been dismissed for controversial speech involve some form of protest or criticism. The occasional nonprotest case should be resolved in accordance with the principles developed in the protest/criticism area. One recent case may illustrate this. Shortly before a controversial referendum among tenants in a particular housing project, the Philadelphia Housing Authority directed its employees not to discuss the issues with the tenants. The rationale for the ruling was to prevent interference with the election and to preserve the impartiality of the Housing Authority during a precarious period. A group of Housing Authority employees, including two who were discharged, brought suit in the federal courts, challenging the constitutionality of the order. The lower court upheld the Housing Authority's position, finding the restraint based upon vital government interests.[71] The court of appeals reversed the decision, however, and found in favor of the employees: "Two factors, in particular . . . have led to a decision in favor of the discharged employees. First, little in the case law supports the imposition of a restraint on all speech of public employees, even concerning a particularized topic. Second, when a prior restraint is sought to be imposed, it should be as narrowly drawn as possible, consistent with the purpose in question."[72]

NOTES

1. See A. Ernest Fitzgerald, "Blowing the Whistle on the Pentagon," in Norman Dorsen and Stephen Gillers, eds., *None of Your Business: Government Secrecy in America* (1974), pp. 251–277. See also *New York Times*, September 19, 1973, p. 1, cols. 6–7; p. 37, col. 1; October 4, 1973, p. 51, col. 4.

2. *Cole v. Richardson*, 405 U.S. 676 (1972).
3. Mass. Gen. Laws ch. 264, § 14.
4. *Law Students Research Council v. Wadmond*, 401 U.S. 154, 192 (1971) (Marshall, J., dissenting); see also *Knight v. Board of Regents*, 269 F. Supp. 339 (S.D.N.Y. 1967), affirmed, 390 U.S. 36 (1968).
5. *Baggett v. Bullitt*, 377 U.S. 360 (1964).
6. Ibid.
7. *Elfbrandt v. Russell*, 384 U.S. 11, 17 (1966).
8. *Shapiro v. Roudebush*, 413 F. Supp. 1177 (D. Mass. 1976).
9. *Baird v. State Bar of Arizona*, 401 U.S. 1 (1971).
10. *New York Times*, September 9, 1976, p. 1, col. 5.
11. 5 U.S.C. § 7532 (1970).
12. *Cole v. Young*, 351 U.S. 536 (1956).
13. 389 U.S. 258 (1967).
14. 5 U.S.C. § 7532(b) (1970).
15. 5 U.S.C. § 7532(a) (1970).
16. *Vitarelli v. Seaton*, 359 U.S. 535 (1959).
17. Exec. Order 10450 § 8(a).
18. Exec. Order 10450 § 7; 5 U.S.C. § 3571, 7312 (1970).
19. *Bruns v. Pomerlau*, 319 F. Supp. 58 (D. Md. 1970).
20. *Cramp v. Board of Public Instruction*, 368 U.S. 278 (1961).
21. *Keyishian v. Board of Regents*, 385 U.S. 589 (1967).
22. *United States v. Brown*, 381 U.S. 437 (1965).
23. *Baggett v. Bullitt*, 377 U.S. 360, 379–80 (1964).
24. *Shelton v. Tucker*, 364 U.S. 479 (1960).
25. *Torcaso v. Watkins*, 367 U.S. 488, 495 (1961).
26. *Kirkley v. Maryland*, 381 F. Supp. 327 (D. Md. 1974).
27. *McDaniel v. Paty*, No. 76-1427, United States Supreme Court.
28. *Trans World Airlines, Inc. v. Hardison*, 432 U.S. — (1977).
29. *Johnson v. United States Postal Service*, 364 F. Supp. 37 (N.D. Fla. 1973).
30. *United States v. City of Albuquerque*, 545 F.2d 110 (10th Cir. 1976).
31. 391 U.S. 563 (1968).
32. 5 U.S.C. § 652(a) (1970).
33. *Meinhold v. Taylor*, 89 Nev. 56, 506 P.2d 420 (1973).
34. *Gilbertson v. McAllister*, 403 F. Supp. 1 (D. Conn. 1975).
35. *Meehan v. Macy*, 392 F.2d 822, modified, 425 F.2d 469 (D.C. Cir. 1968). See also *Kannisto v. City and County of San Francisco*, 541 F.2d 841 (9th Cir. 1976).
36. *Brukiewa v. Police Commissioner*, 257 Md. 36, 263 A.2d 210 (1970).
37. *Muller v. Conlisk*, 429 F.2d 901 (7th Cir. 1970).

38. *Belshaw v. City of Berkeley,* 246 Cal. App. 2d 493, 54 Cal. Rptr. 727 (1966).
39. *Pickering v. Board of Education,* 391 U.S. 563, 570 (1968).
40. *E. g., Fuentes v. Roher,* 519 F.2d 379 (2d Cir. 1975).
41. *Pickering v. Board of Education,* 391 U.S. 563, 572 (1968).
42. *Pickering v. Board of Education,* 36 Ill. 2d 568, 584, 22 N.E.2d 1, 10 (1966) (Schaeffer, J., dissenting).
43. *Brukiewa v. Police Commissioner,* 257 Md. 36, 263 A.2d 210, 218 (1970).
44. *Murray v. Blatchford,* 307 F. Supp. 1038 (D.R.I. 1969).
45. *Goldwasser v. Brown,* 417 F.2d 1169 (D.C. Cir. 1969).
46. *Meehan v. Macy,* 392 F.2d 822, 833 (D.C. Cir. 1968).
47. *Gilbertson v. McAllister,* 403 F. Supp. 1 (D. Conn. 1975).
48. *Puentes v. Board of Education,* 24 N.Y.2d 996, 999, 250 N.E.2d 232, 233, 302 N.Y.S.2d 824, 826 (1969).
49. *Chase v. Fall Mountain Regional School District,* 330 F. Supp. 388 (D.N.H. 171); *Jones v. Battles,* 315 F. Supp. 601 (D. Conn. 1970).
50. *Brubacker v. Board of Education,* 502 F.2d 973 (7th Cir. 1974). See also *Keefe v. Geanakos,* 418 F.2d 359 (1st Cir. 1969); *Parducci v. Rutland,* 316 F. Supp. 352 (M.D. Ala. 1970).
51. *Duke v. North Texas State University,* 338 F. Supp. 990, 997 (E.D. Tex. 1971); cf. *Vogel v. Washington Metropolitan Area Transit Authority,* 533 F.2d 13, 16 (D.C. Cir. 1976).
52. *Abbott v. Thetford,* 529 F.2d 695 (5th Cir. 1976).
53. *Abbott v. Thetford,* 534 F.2d 1101 (5th Cir. 1976).
54. *Waters v. Peterson,* 495 F.2d 91 (D.C. Cir. 1973).
55. *Bullock v. Mumford,* 509 F.2d 384 (D.C. Cir. 1974).
56. *Phillips v. Adult Probation Department, City and County of San Francisco,* 491 F.2d 951 (9th Cir. 1974).
57. *James v. Board of Education,* 461 F.2d 566 (2d Cir. 1972).
58. *Russo v. Central School District No. 1,* 469 F.2d 623 (2d Cir. 1972).
59. *Blevins v. University of North Carolina,* No. C-21-D-70 (M.D.N.C. September 8, 1971).
60. *Pickering v. Board of Education,* 391 U.S. 563, 572 n.4 (1968).
61. *Meehan v. Macy,* 392 F.2d 822, 838-39 (D.C. Cir. 1968); cf. *Huff v. Secretary of the Navy,* 413 F. Supp. 863, 869-70 (D.D.C. 1976).
62. *Klein v. Civil Service Commission,* 260 Iowa 1147, 1157, 152 N.W.2d 195, 201 (1967).
63. *Swaaley v. United States,* 376 F.2d 857 (2d Cir. 1967).

64. *Alfred A. Knopf, Inc. v. Colby,* 509 F.2d 1362 (4th Cir. 1975).
65. *New York Times,* January 2, 1976, p. 8, col. 3. See, for an account of the litigation, *Fitzgerald v. United States Civil Service Commission,* 407 F. Supp. 380 (D.D.C. 1975), reversed on another ground, 554 F. 2d 1187 (D.C. Cir. 1977).
66. *New York Times,* April 30, 1975, p. 10, cols. 4–8.
67. *New York Times,* June 26, 1977, § I, p. 38, cols. 5–6.
68. *Mt. Healthy City School District Board of Education v. Doyle,* 429 U.S. 274 (1977).
69. 5 U.S.C. § 7501(a) (1970).
70. *Arnett v. Kennedy,* 416 U.S. 134 (1974).
71. *Alderman v. Philadelphia Housing Authority,* 365 F. Supp. 350 (E.D. Pa. 1973).
72. *Alderman v. Philadelphia Housing Authority,* 496 F.2d 164 (3rd Cir. 1974).

IV

Politics, Patronage, and Unions

Few public policy issues have been more controversial than the role of government employees in politics. For nearly a century, most federal workers have been barred from active partisan involvement. In 1940, Congress embodied such restrictions in the Hatch Act, which has been a continuing object of controversy.[1] The constitutionality of this law has been challenged frequently and was twice upheld by the Supreme Court.[2] After the second decision, public employee organizations turned from the courts back to Congress and began a concerted attempt to secure repeal. In spring 1976, Congress voted to reduce sharply the range of prohibited political activity,[3] but President Ford vetoed the repeal[4] and the veto stood.[5] Undaunted, the opponents turned next to the Democratic National Convention, where the party platform was amended on the floor to urge repeal of the Hatch Act. The courts have not been the only battleground in this long and intense struggle. But the legal decisions are the major element to which we will give our attention in this chapter.

Which public employees are covered by the Hatch Act restrictions?

The Hatch Act applies to all federal employees in the executive branch of the federal government, whether or not they are in the Civil Service.[6] The law also applies to certain employees of state and local governments whose principal work is in a department funded wholly or partially by federal funds.[7] Persons employed by federally assisted educational or research institutions, or by religious, philanthropic, or cultural organizations are not affected by the Hatch Act.[8] Also excluded from the reach of the law are people paid from appropriations for the Office of the President, the heads and assistant heads of executive departments, people appointed by the President with the advice and consent of the Senate who engage in major policy determinations, and certain administrators of the District of Columbia.[9]

What activities are forbidden by the Hatch Act?

The language of the act makes it unlawful for a federal employee "to use his official authority or influence for the purpose of interfering with an election or affecting the result thereof."[10] The law continues: "No officer or employee [covered by the act] . . . shall take any active part in political management or political campaigns." Such language does not, by itself, give clear guidance to federal employees contemplating involvement in politics. The Hatch Act does not detail the prohibitions, but rather incorporates by reference some 3,000 prior rulings of the Civil Service Commission. These rulings have been periodically codified by the commission, and the Supreme Court has found this practice sufficient, even though Congress has never approved the summary of the activities prohibited by these rulings through the Hatch Act.[11]

Federal employees who are covered by the Hatch Act may not use official authority to influence the outcome of an election, nor may they take any active part in the management or conduct of a political campaign. Specifically, they may not be candidates for or hold office in any national, state, or local partisan political organization; leadership in such an organization is prohibited even if the particular role seems remote from political activity, but may be considered a part of the overall political function of the organization. A federal employee may not solicit funds, directly or indirectly, for partisan political purposes, or organize or promote fund raising for a political cause. Federal employees may not themselves be partisan candidates for elected office; even passive acquiescence in a campaign organized by their friends may be considered a violation of the Hatch Act. Nor may a federal employee endorse or oppose any partisan candidate in a political advertisement, nor circulate a partisan nominating petition.[12]

These are the broad constraints currently applicable to *federal* employees under the Hatch Act. Until recently, the same rules applied to state and local employees on federally funded projects. In 1974, Congress exempted state and local employees from the restrictions on participation in or direction of political campaigns.[13] Thus a federally funded state or local employee is now forbidden only to use official authority to influence the outcome of an election—for example, by threatening to withhold promotion or otherwise coercing subordinates into supporting or opposing a particular candidate. A state or local employee still may not coerce other employees to contribute to a party or candidate. Nor may such a person serve as a partisan candidate for elective public office. Most other activities denied to federal employees are no longer forbidden by federal law to state and local employees.

What political activities are permitted to federal employees?

The statute says only that "all such persons shall re-

tain the right to vote as they may choose and to
express their opinions on all political subjects and candidates."[14] The precise scope of permissible political activity has been partially defined by court decisions and
Civil Service Commission rulings. A person may regis-
ter and vote in a partisan primary as well as a general
election without fear of reprisal. Individual opinions on
political issues may be expressed publicly and pri-
vately. Political posters, badges, buttons, and other
symbols may be displayed. Federal employees may belong to political organizations, so long as they do not
assume a leadership role. They may attend political
gatherings, provided there is no public display of par-
tisanship. A federal employee may freely contribute
money to any candidate or party (subject, of course, to
the new limits of the Federal Election Campaign Act).
A covered employee may even hold certain minor
elected offices, such as justice of the peace, notary public, election judge or commissioner, and may serve on
local school or library boards and public governing
boards for charitable and educational functions of state
and local government.[15]

The major thrust of the Hatch Act is against *partisan* politics. Thus federal employees have broader
latitude with respect to nonpartisan activity and expression. An election is regarded as nonpartisan if none
of the candidates represents a party for which a
presidential elector received votes in the previous
presidential election, regardless of whether sides are
taken on major public issues. Under such conditions, a
federal employee may seek a nonpartisan office, and
may take a more active role in a nonpartisan political
organization than is permitted in a regular political
party.

The activities allowed to state and local employees
since 1974 under federal law are substantially broader.
Under the amended Hatch Act, even those who work
on federally funded projects may, for example, hold office as well as membership in political organizations;

may run for partisan offices, make speeches or solicit voters in support of or in opposition to a partisan candidate, may originate and sign nominating petitions for partisan candidates, may drive voters to the polls, and may (without coercion or intimidation) solicit contributions on behalf of partisan causes or candidates. (An important caution: There may be *state* or *local* *laws,* which will be discussed later in this chapter, that are more restrictive than the present federal restraints. We have summarized here only the Hatch Act provisions that apply to state and local workers on federally funded projects.)

What special rules apply to federal employees in areas where a majority of people hold federal jobs?

At the discretion of the Civil Service Commission, the Hatch Act prohibitions may be modified in areas populated primarily by federal government employees.[16] In such designated areas, a federal worker may be an independent candidate for office even in a partisan election, and may support or oppose such independent candidates. Political activity must not, however, interfere with the employees' primary responsibility to the federal government, and must not create a conflict of interest.

How do the Hatch Act restrictions affect the constitutional rights of public employees?

The Hatch Act curtails the expression and political activity of federal workers to a greater degree than would be valid for the population at large. To that extent, people in the federal service undeniably sacrifice First Amendment freedoms as a condition of employment. Shortly after the Hatch Act was adopted by Congress, a group of federal employees brought suit to challenge the constitutionality of the new law. When the case reached the Supreme Court, most of the claims were rejected as premature because the plaintiffs had not actually done the things they feared might cost them their jobs. But the Court did reach the constitutional issue in the case of one person who had engaged in forbidden political activity and had been threatened with dismissal. On the merits, the Court held that Government could abridge rights of expression to the extent the Hatch Act did since there were overriding interests which outweighed those of the employee wishing to take part in politics.

The Court agreed that citizens not employed by the federal government would be free to engage in such activity. Moreover, the activity occurred on the employee's free time and did not directly interfere with his government job as a roller in the Philadelphia mint. But the Court felt that the desire of Congress to keep partisan politics out of the Civil Service and to protect public workers from political coercion was a strong one: "Evidently what Congress feared was the cumulative effect on employee morale of political activity by all employees who could be induced to participate actively." That fear, concluded the majority, justified the curtailment of First Amendment freedoms. The Court did go on to point out, however, that the Hatch Act "leaves untouched full participation by employees in political decisions at the ballot box and forbids only the partisan activity of federal personnel deemed offensive to efficiency."[17]

Twenty years later, another suit challenged the constitutionality of the Hatch Act. The district court felt that both the governing law and the times had changed sufficiently that the Supreme Court would reverse itself if given a chance. The trial judge thus held the law unconstitutional, chiefly because of the confusion created by the more than 3,000 applicable Civil Service Commission rulings.[18] Thus, the court concluded,

> There is no standard. No one can read the Act and ascertain what it prohibits. . . . Thus do generalized, vague prohibitions become misunderstood and misapplied and serve to limit expression

by millions of Federal Government employees, and their families, in a society where political speech and uninhibited, robust, wide-open debate on public issues are at the essence of self-government.[19]

Surprisingly, however, the Supreme Court majority adhered to its original position and once again sustained the Hatch Act. The Court reaffirmed "the judgment of history . . . that it is in the best interest of the country, indeed essential, that federal service should depend upon meritorious performance rather than political service, and that the political influence of federal employees and others and on the electoral process should be limited."[20] While the evils of the nineteenth-century spoils system might seem more remote than at the time the original prohibitions were enacted, Congress had declined to repeal or substantially alter the law over the years. On balance, the strong government interest in ensuring the neutrality of the federal service (and the appearance of neutrality) outweighed the interest of the individual employee in pursuing politics. Finally, the Supreme Court was less concerned than the trial court about the uncertain situation of the employee, since the Civil Service Commission had from time to time codified and clarified the Hatch Act's prohibitions and permissions. Even if some civil servants might be unclear about what they could and could not do, the Court maintained that "there seems to be little question in the minds of the plaintiffs who brought this lawsuit as to the meaning of the law."[21]

Shortly after this decision in 1973, the battle scene shifted back to Congress. The following year, as part of the package of post-Watergate election reforms, most of the prohibitions against state and local workers were removed from the Hatch Act. Two years later, Congress voted to modify drastically the Hatch Act provisions, to forbid only such "hard core" activity as coercion and intimidation, and partisan conduct while on duty. Virtually all other activities, partisan as well as nonpartisan, would be permitted.[22] President Ford had warned that he would veto such revisions, and he did so, noting that "the public business of our Government must be conducted without the taint of partisan politics" and that "politicizing the civil service is intolerable."[23] Congress failed to override the veto, and the Hatch Act remained in force.[24]

What procedure is used to punish a Hatch Act violation?

The Hatch Act is enforced for federal employees (as well as interpreted) by the Civil Service Commission. When the commission learns of an apparent violation, it will investigate, after notifying the agency for which the suspect works. If the commission feels the matter is worth pursuing, it will send a letter of formal charges to the employee, at least 30 days before any sanction is to take effect. The employee may respond within 15 days; the failure to respond permits the sanction to occur. If the employee does respond, the matter will go to a hearing, unless the employee waives his or her right to a hearing.[25] (The procedures for such hearing are discussed in greater detail in Chapter VII). The penalty for an employee found to have violated the Hatch Act is usually removal from federal service, unless the commission unanimously finds that a lesser penalty is warranted. In no case may the penalty be less than suspension for 30 days.

A slightly different procedure is used for suspected Hatch Act violations by state or local employees. If a hearing examiner decides that no violation occurred or that a discharge would be unwarranted, that decision becomes final unless within 30 days the Civil Service Commission agrees to review the case. If the hearing examiner finds against the employee, commission review is mandatory. If the employee is discharged, and is then reemployed within 18 months in an agency of the same state or municipality, the commission may order withheld from the employing agency federal funds equal to two years' salary for the offending employee at the rate at the time of discharge.[26]

May an employee obtain advice on the legality of proposed political activity?

Yes. Any federal (or covered state or local) employee who wishes a ruling on the legality of a proposed political activity may write to the Office of the General Counsel, Civil Service Commission, Washington, D.C. 20415.

What constitutional rights do state and local government employees have in regard to political activity apart from those covered in the Hatch Act?

Many states, counties, and cities have adopted "little Hatch Acts" covering political activities in government service. Sometimes the provisions are substantially identical to those of the federal Hatch Act; in light of the two U.S. Supreme Court decisions, such provisions would appear to be constitutionally valid. Other state and local laws are, however, somewhat broader and have been challenged in the courts more successfully. The California Supreme Court has announced a strict constitutional standard that must be followed in such cases: "A government agency which would require a waiver of constitutional rights as a condition of public employment must demonstrate: (1) that the political restraints rationally relate to the enhancement of the public service; (2) that the benefits which the public gains by the restraints outweigh the resulting impairment of constitutional rights, and (3) that no alternatives less subversive of constitutional rights are available."[27] Under this test, the California court held that a public hospital nurse had been unconstitutionally discharged for distributing literature and circulating petitions in a campaign to recall the hospital district board. The ban on which the dismissal was based covered a broad range of activity, and in the court's view chilled the exercise of constitutional freedoms by public employees. This concluding comment is instructive:

> As the number of persons employed by government and governmentally assisted institutions continues to grow, the necessity of preserving for them the maximum practicable right to participate in the political life of the republic grows with it. Restrictions on public employees which, in some or all of their applications, advance no compelling public interest commensurate with the waiver of constitutional rights which they require imperil the continued operation of our institutions of representative government.[28]

May state and local employees be barred from running for office?

Several courts have invalidated laws forbidding public employees from seeking elective office. Over a decade ago, the California and Oregon Supreme Courts found that such laws abridged First Amendment freedoms to a far greater degree than was justified to prevent actual conflicts of interest or disruption of public service.[29] Several years later, a federal court of appeals reached a similar conclusion with regard to a Cranston, Rhode Island, city charter provision that required the dismissal of any city employee who became a candidate for nomination or election to public office.[30] The court noted that candidacy for office was an especially strong form of expression, and one for which public employees were well suited. Thus any law that restricted candidacy must be reviewed with special care, since it affected a "fundamental" human right. The court acknowledged that the city had a strong interest in "maintaining the honesty and impartiality of its public work force," but concluded that this interest could be served by requiring candidates to take leaves of absence during the campaign, rather than dismissing them outright. The city's interests might also be served by a narrower restriction, for example, reaching only those employees "whose positions make them vulnerable to corruption and conflicts of interest."[31] If particular abuses of office were shown during a campaign, the city could punish the offender directly. Thus, because of the strength of the individual freedoms and the availability of less restrictive government safeguards, the court found the charter provision unconstitutional.

In certain circumstances, however, running for office may warrant the dismissal of a public employee. In a recent and important case, the federal court of appeals for the Seventh Circuit (a court long sensitive to employee first amendment claims) held that a deputy city attorney was validly dismissed when he announced his candidacy for Congress. The court felt that campaigning for an elective office, even though not that of his superior, undermined an essential relationship of trust and loyalty. The deputy must thus make a choice between retaining his sensitive position on the legal staff and running for Congress.[32]

Other courts have been less sympathetic, and have upheld laws against running for office. The Florida Supreme Court held in 1961 that a law professor could be dismissed for violating the law against seeking elective office.[33] A federal court in Wisconsin in 1969 upheld a law forbidding members of certain agency staffs from seeking partisan offices.[34] The Minnesota Supreme Court held that the legislature has a substantial interest in checking "the evils which necessarily follow when officers or employees in the classified service of the state are permitted to engage in political activity to the extent of running for office."[35] This court felt that such a campaign would divert time, energy, and attention from the employee's primary responsibilities.

Can a public employee be required to take a leave of absence in order to seek elective office?

Yes. Several courts have squarely so held.[36] The federal court in the Rhode Island case observed that a mandatory leave-without-pay policy offered the city a narrower means of serving its legitimate interests.[37] Such a rule would require that an employee campaign on his or her own time and thus reduce the risks of compromise, conflict, and exploitation, while solving the dilemma created by uncertain election prospects.

May a public employee be barred from running against a direct superior?

This issue is not fully settled. Surely such a narrow restriction would be valid where rules against seeking *any* public office have been sustained. The California Supreme Court, in striking down broad city charter provisions against all political candidacy, observed that "a strong case . . . can . . . be made for the view that permitting a public employee to run or campaign against his own superior has so disruptive an effect on the public service as to warrant restriction."[38] Two years later, the same court asked, however, whether the relationship between the hospital nurse and the elected board might not be "so immediate" that the nurse's involvement in a recall campaign would warrant sanctions.[39] Moreover, the "expertise" factor would seem to favor permitting campaigns against superiors; the individual's interest in political expression (and the general public's interest in allowing the individual that freedom) may be strongest in the very same agency or branch of government. On balance, however, courts have been persuaded to uphold such restrictions by the risk of direct conflict between superior and subordinate during a heated political campaign.

May a person be denied public employment on the basis of political party membership?

For most positions in the public service, the answer is no. Throughout American history, party affiliation has been used as a basis for appointment to and dismissal from the roughly half of all government jobs that were not protected by the Civil Service. Until very recently that practice—often called patronage dismissal—was simply taken for granted. When a new party came to power, hundreds of jobs would turn over, and members of the "out party" simply expected to be replaced. Patronage dismissals may take many forms. Most common is the simple discharge of all persons who belong to the "out" party at the time a new party takes control. Some office holders may be dismissed (or denied employment) because they lack the sponsorship of the regular party organization, regardless of their formal affiliation. Others may be asked to contribute money to the "in" party, to work for the election of its candidates, or to support that party in other ways. In subtler fashion, employees may be "invited" to change party affiliation or support, with a high risk that the failure to heed the invitation will result in loss of employment.

Starting in the early 1970s, the victims of patronage dismissal have increasingly sought protection from the courts. The results have varied considerably,[40] and an issue of such importance was destined for the Supreme Court. Late in June 1976, the Court held in *Elrod v. Burns* that most public employees may not be discharged solely on the basis of political party affiliation (or lack of it).[41] The Court stressed the impact of patronage practices on the First Amendment freedoms of the public employee:

An individual who is a member of the out-party maintains affiliation with his own party at the risk of losing his job. He works for the election of his party's candidates and espouses its policies at the same risk. The financial and campaign assistance that he is induced to provide to another party furthers the advancement of that party's policies to the detriment of his own party's views and ultimately his own beliefs, and any assessment of his salary is tantamount to coerced belief. . . . Even a pledge of allegiance to another party, however ostensible, only serves to compromise the individual's true beliefs. Since the average public employee is hardly in the financial position to support his party and another, or to lend his time to two parties, the individual's ability to act according to his beliefs and to associate with others of his political persuasion is constrained, and support for his party is diminished.[42]

In addition to the effects on the individual employee, the Court expressed concern about the effect of patronage dismissals on the quality of the entire Civil Service:

Conditioning public employment on partisan support prevents support of competing political interests. Existing employees are deterred from such support, as well as the multitude seeking jobs. As government employment, state or federal, becomes more pervasive, the greater the dependence on it becomes, and therefore the greater becomes the power to starve political opposition by commanding partisan support, financial and otherwise. Patronage thus tips the electoral process in favor of the incumbent party, and where the practice's scope is substantial relative to the size of the electorate, the impact on the process can be significant.[43]

The Court then recalled the lesson of the loyalty oath decisions—that a person could not be denied public employment for belonging to a particular political group, a precept that should apply at least as much to Republicans and Democrats as to Communists and Ku Klux Klansmen. The Court assessed several interests alleged to justify patronage dismissals—promoting the efficiency of government, giving political parties a strong incentive to succeed, ensuring the loyalty of public workers, and preserving the democratic process.

To these claims, the Court offered several responses: First, in some ways patronage actually hindered, rather than aided, the effective working of government. Second, patronage was not the only means available—and surely not the one least harmful to individual liberties—to serve valid government goals. Third, to the extent that there was a genuine need for loyalty in government, that need could be met by allowing patronage in those "policy-making positions" where the loyalty issue was critical. Thus the Court concluded that most patronage dismissals violated basic First Amendment rights of public employees, unjustified by countervailing government interests.

What "policy-making" positions are still subject to patronage?

The Supreme Court recognized that "no clear line can be drawn between policy-making and nonpolicy-making positions." The key determinant was "the nature of the responsibilities," rather than simply the level of the position in the structure. Consideration should also be given, said the Supreme Court, to "whether the employee acts as an adviser or formulates plans for the implementation of broad goals." The Court added that the burden would rest on the government to show that a particular position was "policy-making" and thus subject to patronage; doubtful cases would be resolved in favor of the employee.

Lower-court decisions offer limited guidance on this issue. Certain cases are relatively clear at opposite poles, such as the unskilled Pennsylvania state highway workers at the nonpolicy-making end,[44] and the independent manager of a West Virginia state liquor store at the policy-making end.[45] (In the latter case, the court was persuaded to decide against the manager by the fact that state liquor control was a sensitive, nonroutine task requiring judgment and discretion.) Also at the policy-making end of the scale were the executive staff members of the Indiana State Department of

Education, who exercised broad discretion and judgment in reviewing and approving federal grant applications and drafting a state education plan.[46] An easy case at the other end of the scale was that of the Illinois state capitol custodian, who clearly made little policy.[47] Perhaps the closest case to date has been the status of the plaintiffs (Illinois deputy sheriffs) in the case that went to the Supreme Court—an issue that the appellate court had sent back for trial at the time the Supreme Court took over the constitutional question.[48]

It may still be too soon after the *Elrod* decision to know just where the line will now fall. The early cases in the lower federal courts seem to have defined the exempt class of "policy making positions" rather broadly.[49] The exception for *Elrod's* safeguards has reached rather far down into the public service corps, and does not always seem to reflect a critical need for loyalty, confidence or consistency.

One other constitutional context may furnish some guidance. In 1959, the Supreme Court held that certain high federal officials enjoyed complete immunity from libel or slander suits because they held "policy-making" positions.[50] The Court felt that persons of such high rank and responsibility should be able to issue statements without fear of civil liability. While the patronage issue is not precisely the same, the courts might find this analogy useful in deciding where to draw the critical line.

What rights does a policy-making employee have regarding political affiliation?

Even a policy-maker may not be required to change political registration, or profess public support, or vote for candidates of the opposite party. Such conditions would violate First Amendment freedoms of expression and belief. At the same time, a policy-maker could presumably be dismissed for belonging to the "wrong" party, could be asked to contribute to the party now in power, or could be "invited" to change party affiliation, with the understanding that dismissal might follow the failure to accept the "invitation." The Supreme Court has made clear, however, that the agency bears the burden of proving that a particular position is a "policy-making" one, and the individual employee receives the benefit of the doubt on this critical issue.[51]

May a dismissal be challenged on patronage grounds if no political reason is given?

Like any new right, the protection against patronage dismissals may not always be readily available. Easy cases can be imagined at both extremes: If all the Republicans are fired the day after a new Democratic governor takes office, and all the Democrats are retained, the inference of a political motive would be inescapable even without any mention of patronage. On the other hand, if only a few persons from one party are fired, or if some from each party receive similar treatment, or if the claimed interest in governmental economy is genuine, it may be a very different matter. The motivations for changes in government personnel are often complex.[52] When a new governor or mayor decides to alter the mission or focus of a department, and fires many of its old staff, politics probably plays some role in the shift. Yet it may be unfair to attribute the purge to patronage as such, even though most of the people hired may be of the "in" party and most of those dismissed of the "out" party. In such cases, courts will probably hold that the individual has the initial burden of proving that the dismissal was politically motivated—a burden that may sometimes be hard to meet. If that burden is met, it is up to the agency to show, if it can, that politics properly played a role because of the policy-making nature of the position and the need for loyalty.

Does the patronage dismissal decision affect people in the Civil Service?

Not directly. One of the major historic reasons for

establishing the Civil Service was to insulate government employment from patronage and the spoils system. Eligibility for classified positions may not be
based on party affiliation, and political contributions
may not be sought from civil servants. The Supreme
Court decision has, in effect, extended similar protections, as a matter of constitutional law, to the unclassi-
fied sector. Should the Civil Service protection fail for
any reason, a person holding a nonpolicy-making position could presumably claim constitutional protection
against political reprisal or coercion. Usually, however,
a constitutional remedy would be unnecessary for
people in the classified service. And for civil servants
holding "policy-making" positions, the constitutional
remedy would be unavailable.

Does a public employee have a right to join a labor organization?

Yes, even if the organization advocates unlawful
strikes. A federal court of appeals held that teachers
had been unconstitutionally dismissed for being members of a labor union. Such activity, said the court, was
within the teacher's freedom of association.[53] Even if
the union actually engaged in illegal activity, such as
strikes, that fact could not penalize individual union
members. Another federal court held that police officers in Washington, D.C., could not be barred from
joining a union that advocated illegal strikes: "Clearly,
this sweeping restriction on a policeman's right to join
others in advocating protected ideas and conduct cannot stand."[54] The court conceded that the government
had a valid interest in preventing strikes by essential
personnel; the remedy, however, was "not to destroy
freedom of association" but rather "to determine
whether proposed concerted activity actually endangers
a valid state interest and if so, to fashion *precise* legislation to protect the public."[55]

The courts have extended the protection beyond
mere union membership. Public employees may assume

leadership roles in such organizations, may recruit new members, may represent the union in dealing with the public and the employer. A teacher, one court has observed, "may not be denied a teaching contract because of his actions in a professional association, regardless of how vigorous they are."[56]

Do public employees have a right not to join a union?

In the sense of being forced to become full members of a union, the answer is almost certainly yes. In May, 1977, however, the Supreme Court held that public employees could be required to pay dues to a union which had been recognized as the exclusive bargaining agent for the unit in which they were employed. Even a conscientious desire not to support the union could not relieve the employees of an obligation (if imposed under state law) to pay union dues. Individual employees were, however, entitled either to have a portion of their dues refunded, or to seek an injunction against union support of particular causes and activities which were abhorrent to them.[57] In this respect, the Supreme Court has simply assimilated the rights of public employees to those earlier recognized for persons in private employment.

Can a public employee insist that union dues be withheld from his or her paycheck?

No. The precise issue was resolved against the union and employees by the Supreme Court in spring 1976. The case was brought by a firefighters' union against the city of Charlotte, North Carolina, which provided a "check off" for employee contributions to savings plans, retirement programs and certain charitable causes. The city refused, however, to withhold union dues, drawing the line at programs of "general interest" in which all city or departmental employees could participate. Moreover, the city argued that public employee collective bargaining was in violation of state law. The Supreme Court unanimously rejected the union's claim and held that the classification among organizations for check-off purposes was a rational one, which sufficed.[58] The fact that the Court made no mention of First Amendment interests suggests that the constitutional right to join a union does not extend to the means by which membership fees are collected.

Can supervisors or administrators be barred from unions to which rank-and-file employees belong?

The few cases appear to be in conflict. Some years ago, a federal court in Florida held unconstitutional a law preventing administrators and supervisors from belonging to a union that represented regular classroom teachers.[59] Such a prohibition, the court held, denied both equality and freedoms of expression and association.

In 1975, however, a federal court in Illinois held that a Chicago suburb could prevent the captains and lieutenants of the fire department from joining the same union as rank-and-file firefighters.[60] The court recognized the First Amendment freedoms involved, but gave priority to the town's interest in discipline, and the need to prevent conflicts of interest between officers and firefighters. The court also pointed to other legislation, including the federal and New York state labor laws, that required the separation of supervisors and supervised workers.

Do public employees have a right to bargain collectively with their employers?

No, not as a matter of constitutional law. Roughly half the states have statutes that provide for bargaining. The federal government, through Executive Order 11,491, permits limited bargaining rights to its employees. Where such laws do not exist, and where government agencies are unwilling to bargain voluntarily, the constitutional claim is tenuous. One court has responded: "There is no question that the right of public employees to associate for the purpose of collective bargaining is a right protected by the First and Fourteenth Amendments to the Constitution. . . . But there is no constitutional duty to bargain collectively with an exclusive bargaining agent. Such duty, when imposed, is imposed by statute."[61]

May government bargain with some public employee groups but not with others?

Yes, so long as the distinction has a rational basis. Two recent federal court cases involved selective bargaining rights—offered to certain municipal employees but denied to police officers.[62] Both courts concluded that the police unions could not insist on bargaining simply because the city bargained with other employee groups. Both decisions reflected obvious differences between law enforcement and other types of public employment. A similar result was reached by another recent federal court case, holding that New Hampshire could constitutionally exclude state university faculty members from a general public employee collective bargaining law.[63]

Do public employees have a right to picket peacefully against agency policy?

Yes, within certain limits. Some qualifications may arise from the *Pickering* decision, discussed in Chapter III. However, a basic constitutional right is clearly at stake. In 1968, the California Supreme Court set aside an injunction against picketing by Sacramento social workers. The injunction forbade, among other things, inducing others to participate in demonstrations, or inducing or calling a strike, work stoppage or other concerted activity against the county.[64] Since the decree included some peaceful protest as well as a threatened strike, it invaded freedoms of association and expression. "Even if we assume," said the court, "that all such activity [dissemination of information, etc.] would be properly enjoinable in so far as it advocated a strike by public employees, still a vast area of constitutionally protected activity falls within the wide reach of the ban."[65] Thus the order was held invalid for its excessive breadth. A recent federal court decision concurs in affording first amendment protection to peaceful public employee picketing.[66]

Do public employees have a right to strike?

Not as a matter of constitutional law. The laws of several states do confer such a right on some groups of public employees. The constitutional claim has been raised frequently and rejected consistently, by both federal and state courts. One federal court has recently observed: "It seems clear that public employees stand on no stronger footing in this regard than private employees and that in the absence of a statute, they too do not possess the right to strike."[67] A federal district court has recently held that termination of state university employees for taking part in an illegal strike was permissible, because neither the constitution nor the state law conferred right to strike.[68] Thus, even though public employees do have a constitutional right to join unions and to picket peacefully, a right to strike can come only from a statute or regulation.

What procedural problems face an illegal public striker?

The Supreme Court has recently resolved one important issue in the aftermath of an illegal public employee strike. Two lower courts had held that a school board could not dismiss striking school teachers during negotiations, since the board members had a substantial interest in the outcome and were thus not impartial. The Supreme Court reversed, holding that due process did not require a hearing by a tribunal other than the school board.[69] Members of the board did not have such a personal or institutional stake in the dispute as would taint their judgment. Bias would not be presumed from the fact that the board was an adversary in the strike that precipitated the dismissal of the teachers. The Court also observed: "the Board's decision was only incidentally a disciplinary decision; it had significant governmental and public policy dimensions as well."[70] Given the strength of the government interests in keeping the sanctions within the school system, the Court concluded that such a procedure was valid.

How does collective bargaining affect the general speech rights of public employees?

A Supreme Court decision in December 1976 provides the clearest answer to date. A Wisconsin school teacher who did not belong to the teachers' union was permitted to speak at a school board meeting. Over the union's objection, he argued for the exclusion of a particular clause in the labor contract that was then being negotiated. He read a petition, signed by a number of other teachers, supporting his views. After the contract was signed (omitting the clause that sparked the controversy), the union claimed the board had committed an unfair labor practice by allowing the individual teacher to speak. The Wisconsin Employment Relations Commission held that teachers could be denied the right to speak, even at public meetings, "on matters subject to collective bargaining." The Wisconsin state courts affirmed this order, finding that an individual teacher's petition to the school board posed a "clear and present danger."

The U.S. Supreme Court unanimously reversed this decision.[71] Since the school board meeting was open to the public, and since the individual teacher was not attempting to negotiate, the board could not abridge, on the basis of union membership or nonmembership, the First Amendment rights of citizens to speak. Apart from the individual teacher's expression, which would be infringed by the state labor commission's decree, the Court stated: "Restraining teachers' expressions to the board on matters involving the operation of the schools would seriously impair the board's ability to govern the district."

NOTES

1. 5 U.S.C. § 7324 (1970).
2. *United Public Workers v. Mitchell*, 330 U.S. 75 (1947); *United States Civil Service Commission v. National Association of Letter Carriers*, 413 U.S. 547, 557 (1973).
3. *New York Times*, March 12, 1976, p. 9, cols. 1–8.
4. *New York Times*, April 13, 1976, p. 24, cols. 2–4.
5. *New York Times*, April 30, 1976, p. A-18, col. 3–4.
6. 5 U.S.C. § 7324(a) (1970); 5 C.F.R. 733.101.
7. 5 U.S.C. § 1501; 5 C.F.R. 151.101.
8. 5 U.S.C. § 7324(b) (1970).
9. 5 U.S.C. § 7324(d) (1970).
10. 5 U.S.C. § 7324(a) (1970).
11. *United States Civil Service Commission v. National Association of Letter Carriers*, 413 U.S. 547, 576–81 (1973).
12. 5 C.F.R. 733.121.
13. 88 Stat. 1290 (1974), amending 5 U.S.C. §§ 1501–02 (1970).
14. 5 U.S.C. § 7324(b) (1970).
15. 5 C.F.R. 733.111.
16. 5 U.S.C. § 7327(b) (1970); 5 C.F.R. 733.124; see also *Democratic State Central Committee for Montgomery County v. Andolsek*, 249 F. Supp. 1009 (D. Md. 1966).
17. *United Public Workers v. Mitchell*, 330 U.S. 75, 99, 101 (1947).
18. *National Association of Letter Carriers v. United States Civil Service Commission*, 346 F. Supp. 578 (D.D.C. 1972).
19. Ibid., pp. 582–583.
20. *United States Civil Service Commission v. National Association of Letter Carriers*, 413 U.S. 547 (1973).
21. Ibid., p. 579.
22. *New York Times*, March 12, 1976, p. 9, cols. 1–8.
23. *New York Times*, April 13, 1976, p. 24, cols. 2–4.
24. *New York Times*, April 30, 1976, p. A-18, cols. 3–4.
25. 5 C.F.R. 733.131-137.
26. 5 C.F.R. 151.131-137.
27. *Bagley v. Washington Township Hospital District*, 65 Cal. 2d 499, 501-02, 421 P.2d 409, 411, 55 Cal. Rptr. 401, 403 (1966).
28. 65 Cal. 2d at 510-11, 421 P.2d at 417, 55 Cal. Rptr. at 409.
29. *Fort v. Civil Service Commission*, 61 Cal. 2d 331, 392

P.2d 385, 38 Cal. Rptr. 625 (1965); *Minielly v. State,* 242 Ore. 490, 411 P.2d 69 (1966).

30. *Mancuso v. Taft,* 476 F.2d 187 (1st Cir. 1973). For later cases sustaining narrower restrictions on political activity, see *Perry v. St. Pierre,* 518 F.2d 184 (2d Cir. 1975); *Paulos v. Breier,* 507 F.2d 1383 (7th Cir. 1974).

31. *Mancuso v. Taft,* 476 F.2d 187, 199 (1st Cir. 1973).

32. *Newcomb v. Brennan,* 558 F.2d 825 (7th Cir. 1977).

33. *Jones v. Board of Control,* 131 So. 2d 713 (Fla. 1961).

34. *Wisconsin State Employees Association v. Natural Resources Board,* 298 F. Supp. 339 (W.D. Wis. 1969).

35. *Johnson v. State Civil Service Department,* 280 Minn. 61, 66, 157 N.W.2d 747, 751 (1968).

36. *Chatham v. Johnson,* 195 So. 2d (Miss. 1967).

37. *Mancuso v. Taft,* 476 F.2d 187, 199 (1st Cir. 1973).

38. *Fort v. Civil Service Commission,* 61 Cal. 2d 331, 338, 38 Cal. Rptr. 625, 629, 392 P.2d 385, 389 (1964).

39. *Bagley v. Washington Township Hospital District,* 65 Cal. 2d 499, 511, 55 Cal. Rptr. 401, 408, 421 P.2d 409, 416 (1966).

40. Compare *Illinois State Employees Association v. Lewis,* 473 F.2d 561 (7th Cir. 1972), with *Nunnery v. Barber,* 503 F.2d 1349 (4th Cir. 1974); *Alomar v. Dwyer,* 447 F.2d 482 (2d Cir. 1971).

41. *Elrod v. Burns,* 427 U.S. 347 (1976).

42. Ibid., p. 355.

43. Ibid., p. 356.

44. *American Federation of State, County and Municipal Employees v. Shapp,* 443 Pa. 527, 280 A.2d 375 (1971).

45. *Nunnery v. Barber,* 503 F.2d 1349 (4th Cir. 1974).

46. *Indiana State Employees Association v. Negley,* 365 F. Supp. 225 (S.D. Ind. 1973).

47. *Illinois State Employees Association v. Lewis,* 473 F.2d 561 (7th Cir. 1972).

48. *Burns v. Elrod,* 509 F.2d 1133 (7th Cir. 1975).

49. E.g., *Alfaro de Quevedo v. DeJesus Schuck,* 556 F.2d 591 (1st Cir. 1977); *Committee for the Protection of First Amendment Rights v. Bergland,* 434 F. Supp. 314 (D.D.C. 1977); *Duff v. Sherlock,* 432 F. Supp. 423 (E.D. Pa. 1977); *Rosenberg v. Redevelopment Authority of Philadelphia,* 428 F. Supp. 498 (E.D. Pa. 1977); cf. *Rosenthal v. Rizzo,* 555 F.2d 390 (3d Cir. 1977).

50. *Barr v. Matteo,* 360 U.S. 564 (1959).

51. *Elrod v. Burns,* 427 U.S. 347 (1976).

52. *Vargas v. Barcelo,* 385 F. Supp. 879 (D.P.R. 1974).

53. *McLaughlin v. Tilendis,* 398 F.2d 287 (7th Cir. 1968); *American Federation of State, County and Municipal Employees v. Woodward,* 406 F.2d 137 (8th Cir. 1969).

54. *Police Officers Guild, National Association of Police Officers v. Washington*, 369 F. Supp. 543, 552 (D.D.C. 1973).
55. Ibid., p. 553.
56. *Lee v. Smith*, GERR No. 383, B-15, B-16 (E.D. Va. 1971).
57. *Abood v. Detroit Board of Education*, U.S. 431 (1977) 209.
58. *City of Charlotte v. Firefighters, Local 660*, 426 U.S. 283 (1976)
    lotte v. Firefighters, Local 660, DBF *U.S.* BRC AVTGFQ...
59. *Orr v. Thorp*, 308 F. Supp. 1369 (S.D. Fla. 1969).
60. *Elk Grove Firefighters Local No. 2340 v. Willis*, 400 F. Supp. 1097 (N.D. Ill. 1975).
61. *Indianapolis Education Association v. Lewallen*, 72 LRRM 2071, 2072 (7th Cir. 1969).
62. *Confederation of Police v. City of Chicago*, 529 F.2d 89 (7th Cir. 1976); *Vorbeck v. McNeal*, 407 F. Supp. 733 (E.D. Mo. 1976).
63. *University of New Hampshire Chapter, American Association of University Professors v. Hasleton*, 397 F. Supp. 107 (D.N.H. 1975).
64. In re *Berry*, 68 Cal. 2d 137, 436 P.2d 273, 65 Cal. Rptr. 273 (1968).
65. 68 Cal. 2d at 155–57, 436 P.2d at 285, 65 Cal. Rptr. at 285.
66. *National Treasury Employees Union v. Fasser*, 428 F. Supp. 295 (D.D.C. 1976).
67. *United Federation of Postal Clerks v. Blount*, 325 F. Supp. 879, 883 (D.D.C. 1971); *Johnson v. City of Albany*, 413 F. Supp. 782, 797 (M.D. Ga. 1976).
68. *United Steel Workers v. University of Alabama in Birmingham*, 430 F. Supp. 996 (N.D. Ala. 1977).
69. *Hortonville Joint School District No. 1 v. Hortonville Education Association*, 426 U.S. 482 (1976).
70. Ibid., p. 495.
71. *City of Madison, Joint School District No. 8 v. Wisconsin Employment Relations Commission*, 429 U.S. 167 (1976).

V

The Private Lives of Public Employees

There is a constant tension between the public role and the private life of a government employee. Since the government as an employer is bound by the Constitution, people who work for government have rights not available to employees in the private sector. On the other hand, government agencies often regulate the conduct and appearance of their employees by rules they would not think of applying to the general public. The cases are legion. A person who spent weekends in a nudist colony was denied employment with the Baltimore police department.[1] Teachers in southern states have been fired for sending their children to segregated private schools.[2] A policeman in New York, a postal clerk in San Francisco, and an FBI staff member in Washington were fired for living with women to whom they were not married.[3] Government employees in many states have refused to disclose their financial holdings, or have done so reluctantly in order to keep their jobs.[4] People across the country have been denied employment because of suspected homosexuality.[5] Many of these conflicts have been brought into the courts, and have produced the body of case law that now defines the private rights of public employees.

This chapter is organized under several major headings—"Investigation, Inquiry, and Surveillance"; "Life Style and Privacy in General"; "Grooming, Dress, and Appearance"; "Heterosexual Associations"; and "Homosexual Associations." Choice of residence and the effect of prior criminal record are discussed in Chapter II; private communications are discussed in Chapter III. The material in this chapter does not exhaust the relationship between public employment and private lives.

INVESTIGATION, INQUIRY, and SURVEILLANCE

May an applicant or employee be required to answer questions about private conduct or associations?

In general, yes, although the obligation has major qualifications. Courts have recognized that government has a legitimate interest in inquiring into the fitness of prospective employees. That interest extends to past activities and associations—although, as noted in Chapter III, certain inquiries into *political* affiliations may impermissibly invade First Amendment rights. Even where the agency might not be able to disqualify an applicant for an affirmative answer, courts are inclined to allow the question to be asked if there is a plausible reason for doing so.

The limitations and qualifications are, however, important. First, there must be a rational relationship between the question and the interest of the government as employer. In a major case involving denial of security clearances to suspected homosexuals (who refused to answer intrusive questions), a federal court of appeals held that an agency may not conduct a mere "fishing expedition" into an applicant's private life. "Only information which is reasonably necessary to make a determination" about an applicant's fitness may be demanded.[6] Another court has said that "governmental inquiries must be reasonably calculated to elicit information concerning an applicant's private . . . life which bear directly on his suitability for federal employment."[7]

Second, there must be some legitimate basis for inquiring into the particular area of private conduct. An agency could not, for example, ask every applicant probing questions about sexual activity or involvement; it could ask only those applicants about whom it had some prior information or reasonable suspicion. Otherwise every applicant would be required to disclaim or disprove conduct or affiliation wholly unrelated to the qualifications for the job.

Third, the cases make clear that the interest in privacy extends beyond simply political affiliations. One court has observed that "there is a right under the First Amendment for a person to keep private the details of his sex life."[8] Personal as well as partisan and other political involvement thus enjoys a measure of constitutional protection.

Fourth, the clarity of the questions and the explanation of their intended use may influence the scope of permissible inquiry. A federal court of appeals has warned that "the reasonableness of requiring answers to certain questions may be affected by the clarity and rationality of the policies sought to be effectuated by the questions. Where disclosure is required of circumstances of an intensely personal nature, the discloser is arguably entitled to know the standards by which his revelations will be assessed."[9]

Fifth, the sensitivity of the particular job or position will also affect the scope of inquiry. Questions that may appropriately be asked of an applicant for a key role in the foreign service or secret service would be absurd for a custodian or file clerk. One court has recently held, for example, that an applicant for a State Department post who had admitted seeing a psychiatrist for "anxiety" could be asked other questions about his sex life and drug use; the partial disclosure "furnished a reasonable basis for the agency to explore further the emotional stability [of the applicant] for the sensitive position involved."[10]

Do laws and regulations limit the scope and manner of questions asked of federal employees or applicants?

Yes. As a result of the Privacy Act adopted by Congress in 1974,[11] applicants for federal employment (and current employees) gained substantial protection. This law requires most agencies of the federal government to tell every individual from whom information is required (whether on the application form or on a separate sheet that the individual may retain): (1) the authority on which the request is based, and whether the disclosure sought is voluntary or mandatory under the applicable law; (2) the principal purpose for which the information is intended to be used; (3) the routine uses that may be made of the information (including the category of potential users and the purposes for such use); and (4) the effect on the applicant, if any, of refusing to provide any or all of the information requested. Separate provisions of the Privacy Act[12] require a similar disclosure to accompany agency demands for social security numbers; the individual must be told whether the revelation is mandatory or voluntary, and what use will be made of the number if it is revealed. Thus a person who has (or fears) an adverse record may at least anticipate the consequences of the agency's findings and offer refutation in advance.

Under the Privacy Act, an aggrieved individual may bring a civil action in the federal district courts against an agency for alleged violation of the notice requirements. Damages may be recovered if the court finds that the agency intentionally or willfully misrepresented the reasons for or the intended uses of the requested information.[13]

May an applicant or employee be required to disclose financial data?

Yes. Courts have generally sustained rather broad financial disclosure laws, despite claims of invasion of privacy. After the California Supreme Court struck down such a law because it was not limited to assets and holdings that might create a conflict of interest,[14] other state courts have been less rigorous. Especially in the post-Watergate era, these courts have found a compelling state interest in the required disclosure of the finances not only of elected and appointed officials themselves, but sometimes of members of their families as well. In addition to deterring actual conflicts of interest, such laws "foster a climate of honesty perceptible by the public at large." The Maryland Court of Appeals has explained: "It can hardly be denied that the . . . [government] has a compelling interest, on behalf of its citizens, in ensuring that its public officials and employees act with honesty, integrity, and impartiality in all their dealings and that their private financial holdings and transactions present no conflict of interest between the public trust and private interests."[15] While the Supreme Court has not ruled directly on this issue, it has refused to review two state court decisions upholding conflict of interest laws and recently declined to review a challenge to a city rule requiring all police officers to disclose not only their own assets and income but that of their spouses as well.[16] Moreover, the Supreme Court has recently rejected constitutional claims of privacy in connection with disclosure of income tax, bank, and business records.[17]

The laws that have been sustained are limited to positions in which the public confidence is especially important. There seem to have been few attempts, if any, to require rank-and-file public employees to disclose their assets or outside income. Were such a law enacted, it might fail to meet the tests imposed by the courts, since the public confidence in government is limited chiefly to holders of senior and administrative posts.

May a public employee be required to answer questions about past criminal activity?

Yes. Where the questions are "specifically, directly and narrowly related to the performance of his official duties," the employee may be compelled to respond.[18] The Supreme Court has held, however, that a public employee may not be dismissed for invoking the privilege against self-incrimination when faced with such an inquiry.[19] Nor may a person be discharged for refusing to waive immunity from prosecution in return for testifying.[20] Thus there is an obligation to respond, which the employee cannot avoid; but resort to the privilege against self-incrimination may not be the basis for dismissal.

Presumably, an applicant for public employment enjoys comparable rights. While a government agency may ask relevant questions about past criminal conduct or law violations, an applicant could not be rejected solely for claiming the protection of the privilege against self-incrimination. Resort to the privilege might, of course, later be found to constitute perjury, but that is quite another issue. Moreover, some states have enacted laws permitting applicants to answer no to such questions if their arrests did not result in convictions, and other laws prohibit inquiry by employers (including public agencies) into arrests not leading to convictions. The recent New York statute appears to be the most comprehensive of these laws.[21]

May a public employee or applicant be required to take a polygraph or lie detector test?

The answer is not clear. The extent to which such devices are used in public employment is not known. It was recently revealed, for example, that 60 percent of persons rejected for employment by the Central Intelligence Agency failed to pass lie detector tests.[22] Some agencies routinely use such screening procedures. Their use has been challenged, both because of suspected inaccuracy and because of constitutional concern about potential invasions of privacy. These challenges have produced two types of protection.

The laws of 14 states forbid the use of lie detectors by employers. In other states, the use of such devices is not prohibited outright but is regulated, for example, by requiring the testing and licensing of persons who operate polygraphs. Some of these laws do, however, exempt law enforcement agencies (with respect to employment as well as criminal investigation), and a few even exempt all public agencies, thus reducing the protection for government employees and applicants.

In the courts, challenges to the use of polygraphs and lie detectors have produced varied results. Some courts have simply rejected such challenges, finding no constitutional violation.[23] Other courts have enjoined the use of polygraphs, though not necessarily on constitutional grounds.[24] Where the constitutional issue has been reached, still other courts have struck a middle ground. The Washington Supreme Court, for example, has held that

> if in the exercise of prudent judgment, the investigating authority determines it reasonably necessary to utilize the polygraph examination as an investigatory tool to test the dependability of prior answers of suspected officers to questions specifically, narrowly and directly related to the performance of the official duties, then such investigative authority may properly request such officers to submit to a polygraph test under pain of dismissal for refusal.[25]

The Washington court further tightened the net by defining the "reasonable necessity" as involving a very substantial public interest that warranted extreme investigatory methods—and the gravity of which would be subject to objective review by a court. In earlier cases where the use of polygraphs has been enjoined, the courts stressed the relatively minor nature of the infraction being investigated, and balanced the competing interests in favor of the individual.[26] Cases in which the use of polygraphs has been upheld seem to have involved rather serious crimes.

Given this wide variety of both statutory and decisional law, it is difficult to draw any neat conclusions. In the absence of a protective statute, there is no blanket right for a public employee or applicant to refuse to submit to a polygraph test. However, it may later develop that the basis of the inquiry was tenuous or the suspected infraction so minor as not to warrant the use of such devices. In most cases, however, the courts would probably be inclined to allow the investigation to proceed.

Is the physical privacy of a public employee protected against searches and surveillances?

Yes, to a substantial degree. In the leading case, a federal court of appeals ten years ago held that evidence obtained without a warrant from the off-base quarters of a civilian employee of the Air Force could not be used in a discharge proceeding.[27] The next year, another federal court extended this protection to a search of on-base living quarters of civilian personnel.[28] Both cases clearly recognize that the Fourth Amendment protects public employees against lawless searches and seizures of their homes. On the other hand, several cases dealing with government workers' lockers have been less protective of privacy. In one case, a regulation permitting superiors to search lockers had the effect of waiving the employees' privacy claims.[29] Another case involving the search of a staff member's desk defined a rather limited zone of privacy.[30] The scope of protection of on-the-job facilities such as lockers and desks thus remains uncertain.

The legality of surveillance in the public sector is

also unclear. Undoubtedly a substantial amount of surveillance does exist—whether through tapping of telephones, two-way public address systems, hidden television cameras, and use of undercover agents. There is relatively little law defining the limits of such information-gathering. A 1975 California Supreme Court decision may come closest to the mark. A faculty member at the University of California at Los Angeles brought suit to challenge the use of undercover police agents posing as students, assigned to gather information about suspected campus "radical" activity. The court held that such practices violated the First Amendment liberties of both students and faculty: "Given the delicate nature of academic freedom, we visualize a substantial probability that this alleged covert police surveillance will chill the exercise of First Amendment rights [and] also constitutes a prima facie violation of the explicit 'right of privacy' recently added to our state constitution."[31]

It is difficult to generalize from the California case to other forms of government surveillance. Courts have always had a special concern for academic freedom, and would likely forbid information-gathering practices in the college classroom that might be allowed in the office, the warehouse, or the hospital kitchen. Courts would presumably balance the privacy claims of the individual against the governmental need for the information, weighing such factors as the gravity of the suspected offense, the basis for the suspicion, and the availability of less intrusive ways of obtaining the information.

LIFE STYLE and PRIVACY in GENERAL

Are a public employee's private associations constitutionally protected?

Yes. In Chapter III, we considered the extent to which an employee's or applicant's political associations were protected by the First Amendment. But the constitution clearly goes beyond political affiliations. For example, in the case of *Bruns v. Pomerlau,* a federal district court held that an otherwise qualified applicant could not be rejected for police work simply because he belonged to a nudist organization.[32] After reviewing the discreet nature of the nudist group, and assuring itself that the applicant would be able to enforce laws against indecent exposure, the court concluded that his "private, nonpolitical association with those who espouse nudism should be no less protected than associations of a political nature." In another recent case, a federal court held that a school board may not refuse to hire a teacher for living in an interracial, religious commune.[33] The court concluded that the applicant had been "denied a job because she chose to exercise her constitutionally protected right of free association." After weighing the competing interests, the court found "nothing in the evidence which indicates that the [school board's] interest in keeping [commune] residents out of the school system is more compelling than the protection of the plaintiff's freedom of association."[34]

Such principles are not confined to First Amendment freedom. A recent federal appellate case seriously questioned whether a black Alabama police officer could be dismissed because he allowed two white women employed by a local poverty agency to board with his family.[35] The police department ruled that city employees had to "stay in the middle of the road" in racial matters, and that the officer in question had strayed from the median by taking in the white women. Accordingly, he was forced to resign. When he brought suit, the federal court of appeals held that if the dismissal rested solely on racial grounds, the police agency must prove that such conduct "would materially and substantially impair" the officer's ability to perform police work. Thus racial equality, as well as freedom of association, is within the scope of a public employee's privacy.[36]

Other types of constitutional claims may be less readily recognized. Take, for example, the controversary created by dismissal of certain white southern school teachers for sending their own children to racially segregated private schools.[37] School boards have justified such actions by the obligation to foster desegregation, and the attendant need for teachers to set a good example as parents. Yet such dismissals clearly raise a constitutional issue. Fifty years ago, the Supreme Court held that a state could not abolish all private schools, because parents have a constitutional right to send their children to nonpublic schools if they wish.[38] In terms of the choice issue, the admission policies of the private school should not limit the parental right. Thus one federal district court held such a teacher-parent policy unconstitutional by analogy to policies denying free speech or racial equality to public employees.[39] The court of appeals, in a later case, reached the opposite conclusion.[40] The Supreme Court agreed to hear the case, but then dismissed it several months later because of the adoption of a new state law and a relevant intervening constitutional decision. Chief Justice Burger, in a concurring opinion, cautioned that the Court's action "intimates no view on the question of when, if ever, public school teachers— or any comparable public employees—may be required, as a condition of their employment, to enroll their children in any particular school or refrain from sending them to a school which they, as parents, consider desirable." He concluded: "Few familial decisions are as immune from governmental interference as parents' choice of a school for their children, so long as the school chosen otherwise meets the conditional standards imposed by the State."[41]

Are there limits to government control over other aspects of the public employee's private life?

Yes, although the limits are less clear where no distinct and separate constitutional right is involved. Recent decisions have held that there must be some relationship between the needs of government administration and the private behavior in question. One court has said, "There must be a real and substantial relation between the employee's conduct and the operation by the employee of the public service."[42] Another court has observed that "the governmental regulation of the lawful, off-duty activities of its employees will be subject to close scrutiny, for surely the threat of being fired is equal to that of most . . . criminal sanctions, and the government's interest in off-the-job conduct is minor."[43]

Perhaps the clearest statement of this precept comes from the California Supreme Court decision of *Morrison v. State Board of Education.*[44] The court held that a teacher could not be dismissed for "immoral" or "unprofessional" conduct on the basis of an isolated homosexual involvement. Such a charge, said the court, would disqualify an employee only if "that conduct indicates that the [person] is unfit to teach." The court thus put the issue in a larger context, and found that the teacher's fitness to teach had not been impaired. Since it reached that result by interpreting the state statute, there was no need to decide whether a broad constitutional right of privacy might also apply.

What factors determine the "rational relationship" or "fitness" in a private conduct case?

Many factors may be relevant to this judgment. In the *Morrison* case, the California court suggested that at least the following elements should be weighed:

The likelihood that the conduct may have adversely affected students or fellow teachers; the degree of such adversity anticipated; the proximity or remoteness in time of the conduct; the type of teaching certificate held by the party involved; the extenuating or aggravating circumstances, if any, surrounding the conduct; the praiseworthiness or blameworthiness of the conduct, [and] the likelihood of the recurrence of the questioned conduct.[45]

Other courts have considered additional factors, including the sensitivity of the position held and the way in which the private conduct related to the responsibilities of the position; the way in which the conduct is viewed by society at large (including its status under the criminal laws); the way such activity would be treated by other public agencies and by private employers; any alternatives that could meet the governmental need without abridging the employee's liberty; and the overall record of the employee apart from the suspect activity.[46] Thus the process of judging the legal significance of particular private conduct turns out to be rather complex.

Do public employees have a right to clear warning of private conduct to which the agency objects?

Yes. Several courts have held that the form of such a condition may be as relevant as its substance. Vague language such as "conduct unbecoming" or "behavior inimical to the service" gives the employee little warning as to what is expected.[47] Not only the employee, but the courts as well, need some specific guidance as to what the agency demands of its staff.

A most relevant case is that of Thomas Carter, a bachelor FBI clerk who briefly shared an apartment with a woman to whom he was not married. When he was dismissed for "conduct unbecoming an employee of the Bureau," he successfully sought reinstatement. The court of appeals found that he had not received adequate warning that his behavior might get him into trouble with the Bureau:[48]

> The Government invokes the standard of the lady from Dubuque and argues that . . . it is reasonable to compel moral standards for all employees—clerks as well as agents—that would satisfy that most upright lady. . . . There is a threshold problem, whether the employees have adequate notice of such a standard. . . . [There must be a trial on the issue whether the FBI handbook] clearly puts FBI employees on notice that they must meet not only the general standards of their own community, but also the special standards of the lady from Dubuque.[49]

Other courts have likewise insisted on clarity and precision before commonplace private conduct can be penalized by a public agency.[50] Yet many courts still sustain dismissals based on general language such as "the good of the service."

GROOMING, DRESS, and APPEARANCE

May government forbid its employees to have long hair, beards, or mustaches?

The answer is uncertain in light of the only (and quite recent) Supreme Court decision on the subject. In a number of previous cases, lower courts struck down hair length and style regulations on various constitutional grounds—denial of equal protection, abridgment of freedom of expression, and denial of due process.[51] Such restrictions were occasionally upheld when they related directly to health and safety needs in certain hazardous occupations. In the case that reached the Supreme Court, a group of male police officers challenged the authority of the county to regulate the length and style of their hair. The court of appeals held the regulation unconstitutional, because the "choice of personal appearance is an ingredient of an individual's personal liberty" protected by the Fourteenth Amendment; and because the county had failed "to make the slightest showing of the relationship between its regulation and the legitimate interest it sought to promote." The appellate court conceded that police departments did have special interests in discipline and uniformity, but found insufficient evidence of the need to serve that interest by regulating hair length and style.[52]

The Supreme Court reversed in *Kelley v. Johnson*,[53] decided in April 1976. The Court began by assuming that the Constitution protects a citizen's choice of personal appearance (including hair style). But the claim before the Court was the personal appearance of police officers, and not of ordinary citizens. Since the county regulated many aspects of police conduct, by requiring the wearing of a uniform and saluting the flag, and by forbidding smoking, there were already substantial limits on the officer's personal freedom of choice. The selection of a "particular mode of organization" for law enforcement further constrained the range of individual employee choice. The hair length and style rules "cannot be viewed in isolation, but must be rather considered in the context of the county's chosen mode of organization of its police force."[54] The constitutional issue was thus a rather narrow one: "It is whether [the police officers] can demonstrate that there is no rational connection between the regulation, based as it is on [the county's method of organizing its police force] and the promotion of safety of persons and property." The Court did not have to search far for a negative answer. The county might well have based its regulation of hair styles "on a desire to make police officers readily recognizable to members of the public, or a desire for the *esprit de corps* that such similarity is felt to inculcate within the police force itself."[55] Either interest would provide the necessary rational basis for the regulation. Justice Powell concurred in the decision, but wanted to keep open the issue of "a liberty interest within the Fourteenth Amendment as to matters of personal appearance," and noted that a regulation that might be reasonable for a police force "would be an impermissible intrusion upon liberty in a different context."[56] Justices Brennan and Marshall dissented, arguing that the Constitution protects the personal appearance of public employees, and that the regulations in question did not rationally serve the asserted governmental interests.[57]

It is too early to tell how broadly the *Kelley* decision will affect the regulation of appearance of public employees. The Supreme Court did stress the nature of the particular agency, and posited two governmental interests—recognizability and *esprit de corps*—that would relate rather tenuously to hair length and style in most other public occupations. Moreover, the county police regulation did contain certain exceptions: conforming wigs could be worn, and beards or goatees were permitted "for medical reasons." On the other hand, the *Kelley* case announced a new and rather lax standard of review, which presumably goes well beyond law enforcement agencies: that a regulation of public employees' personal appearance would be struck down only if "no rational connection" with valid public interests could be established. Many lower court decisions that have invalidated hair length and other rules under a stricter standard may now be in doubt.

One qualification is certainly not foreclosed by *Kelley*. Some courts have insisted that government use the least intrusive method of controlling personal appearance even where substantial agency interests existed.[58] If, for example, the health or safety hazards of facial or flowing hair could be controlled by use of hair nets or face masks, such less onerous alternatives have sometimes been required.

Do regulations of hair length and style imposed only on men constitute unlawful sex discrimination?

No. This issue has been raised frequently under Title VII of the 1964 federal Civil Rights Act, which forbids most forms of sex discrimination. (See Chapter VI.) Four federal courts of appeals have held that even though such regulations are imposed only on men, leaving women free to wear longer hair, they do not violate the civil rights laws.[59] No federal appellate court has held to the contrary.

May government regulate a public employee's mode of dress?

Within broad limits, yes. Uniforms are required for many occupations, and in the *Kelley* case the Supreme Court apparently gave its blessing to such rules. Lower courts have held, for example, that police officers may be compelled to wear American flag patches on their sleeves or name tags on their chests, even though free expression is thus curtailed to a degree.[60] In such cases, the governmental interest in recognizability, uniformity, or *esprit de corps* would seem at least as strong as in the *Kelley* case itself.

In occupations requiring less uniformity, dress and grooming requirements have fared less consistently. Some years ago the New York State Commissioner of Education upheld the right of a physical education teacher to wear a bikini while teaching swimming,[61] and an arbitrator held that an elementary teacher could not be forbidden to wear a pantsuit in the classroom.[62] Two recent cases reach somewhat different results, however. A federal court of appeals has held that a public school teacher may be denied reemployment at least partly because of the shortness of her skirts, since her attire was relevant to her responsibility and her "image," and since no constitutional right encompassed skirt lengths.[63] Another federal appellate court has recently rejected a male teacher's claim that he was improperly reprimanded for refusing to wear a tie in class, as he had been ordered by the principal to do.[64] In both cases, the absence of any constitutional right was central to the rather summary dismissal of the teachers' claims.

HETEROSEXUAL ASSOCIATIONS

May a public employee be dismissed for relations with a person of the opposite sex to whom he or she is not married?

The answer depends on the circumstances. At one end of the scale, courts have been sympathetic to bachelors dismissed because they spent a night or two with an unmarried woman friend.[65] At the other end, there is the case of the married California junior college professor who was caught with a female student in a car in the college parking lot, *in flagrante delicto*.[66] Many cases fall between the two extremes, and the results are hard to predict. Certain factors can, however, be identified.

It is significant whether or not the relationship is adulterous, although a single transgression by a married public employee will not necessarily warrant dismissal under the "fitness" test. The openness or notoriety of the conduct is also significant. Two very recent cases sustaining the dismissal of government employees charged with adulterous cohabitation stressed the public visibility of the relationship as a legally significant element.[67] A California case sustained the dismissal of a teacher who not only had taken an active part in a "swingers" club, engaging in intercourse with men other than her husband, but had described her exploits on a Los Angeles television program.[68] (Although she wore a disguise while on the air, her identity was apparent to fellow teachers.) Even under the "fitness" test of the *Morrison* case, the California court found this an instance of "immoral conduct" mainly because the teacher's "performance certainly reflected a total lack of concern for privacy, decorum, or preservation of her dignity and reputation."[69] Finally, the frequency of the conduct undoubtedly affects the judgment of courts under the "fitness" test; in the "swingers" case, the activity continued for a fairly substantial period and involved several other men.

May a person be denied public employment for having a child out of wedlock?

There are widely publicized cases of unmarried teachers who have been dismissed for bearing children, or even for becoming pregnant. The Supreme Court agreed to review one such case in 1976, but then dismissed it without explanation. In that case, the lower federal courts had held unconstitutional a rule barring unwed mothers from employment as teachers. Such a policy "equates the single fact of illegitimate birth with irredeemable moral disease"—a presumption that was "not only patently absurd" but also "mischievous and prejudicial, requiring those who administer the policy to 'investigate' the parental status of school employees and prospective applicants."[70] Moreover, there were alternative means by which valid school interests could be served, notably through holding hearings on specific immoral conduct charges against particular teachers. The court also rejected the school board's claim that such a policy was needed to discourage promiscuity among impressionable female students, since there was no evidence of any such connection. Other recent lower court cases are in conflict, some finding an infringement of the employee's basic rights, others upholding the interests of the school board.[71] Further clarification by higher courts is needed, and probably will be forthcoming.

May a person be denied public employment for changing his or her sex?

Increasing publicity has been given to the status of

public employees who have changed sex, typically from male to female. Occasional dismissals of transsexuals have been challenged, although there appears to be only one reported decision. *In re Grossman* involved a tenured music teacher in New Jersey who, after 14 years of satisfactory service as a man, returned from vacation one spring as a woman, following a sex change operation. The school board first took away the teacher's tenure and later ruled the teacher ineligible for future employment. This decision was upheld by the State Commissioner of Education. The teacher unsuccessfully sought relief both in the state and federal courts and the Supreme Court refused to review the case.[72] Although the number of sex changes having occupational impact seems to be increasing, *Grossman* is apparently the only court decision on the employee's rights following such an operation.

HOMOSEXUAL ASSOCIATIONS

May a person be denied public employment for homosexual conduct?

The answer, again, is that it depends on the situation. On the one hand, increasing numbers of state and local civil rights laws include "sex orientation" among grounds on which discrimination is forbidden. Such provisions forbid denial of employment to homosexuals or dismissal of persons because they are homosexual. Some government agencies, including the New York City Civil Service System, and the police departments of Los Angeles and Washington State, have removed historic bars against the hiring of homosexuals. The federal Civil Service Commission has recently taken similar action, which we will explore below.

Where such laws and policies do not exist, however, the answer is quite uncertain. The California Supreme Court and several federal courts have ruled in favor of dismissed homosexuals, either on constitutional or statutory grounds.[73] The California Supreme Court has, in fact, quite recently reaffirmed its *Morrison* holding in the case of a teacher actually arrested but not convicted for homosexual solicitation.[74] Since the conduct in *Morrison* was not technically criminal, much less the subject of an arrest, some doubt remained about the scope of that decision. The California court has now reaffirmed that such a transgression simply does not constitute "immoral conduct" nor evidence "unfitness to teach."

The constitutional claim of the homosexual employee has, however, recently become attenuated. In spring 1976, the Supreme Court sustained the Virginia sodomy law by summarily affirming a lower court ruling, thus implicitly rejecting the claim that sexual relations between consenting adults fall within a constitutionally protected zone of privacy.[75] This holding appears to remove the major premise of the several decisions that have struck down homosexual disabilities on constitutional grounds. The Supreme Court later refused to review two cases in which lower courts—the federal court of appeals in California[76] and the Supreme Court of Washington[77]—had sustained the disqualification of employees solely on the basis of admitted homosexual relations. When in the fall of 1977 the Court simply declined to review the Washington case involving a Tacoma school teacher, front page headlines implied that the Justices had in fact affirmed the substance of the lower decisions. Such an impression is clearly incorrect; the Supreme Court has consistently avoided reaching the merits of this highly sensitive and divisive issue.

To what extent do statutes and regulations protect the homosexual employee?

The charters or civil rights laws of many communities (among them Detroit, Portland, Minneapolis, Washington, D.C., and Seattle) and numerous university centers (e.g., Bloomington, Madison, Austin,

Berkeley, and Santa Barbara) forbid discrimination in employment on grounds of "sexual orientation" or "sexual preference." Typically, these laws give a remedy to a person denied public employment because of admitted or suspected homosexuality. (See Chapter VI for a discussion of civil rights laws and remedies available under them.)

Most significant is the regulation that was issued by the U.S. Civil Service Commission in July 1975. Reflecting recent court decisions, the regulation provides that a homosexual may be denied employment "only when the notoriety accompanying the conduct can reasonably be expected to adversely affect the person's ability to perform his or her job or the agency's ability to carry out its responsibilities." Thus a person cannot be found unsuitable for federal employment on the basis of "unsubstantiated conclusions concerning possible embarrassment to the Federal service." Instead, "a person may be dismissed or found unsuitable for Federal employment where the evidence establishes that such person's sexual conduct affects job fitness."[78] The commission's decision to adopt the "fitness" test liberalizes a standard under which many otherwise qualified persons had been rejected for, or dismissed from, employment because of homosexual involvement.

Does the public or private nature of homosexuality affect the public employee's rights?

Yes, both under regulations and under court decisions. The new Federal Civil Service ruling clearly excludes from protection the situation in which "notoriety" may impair either the individual's fitness or the agency's position. Court decisions, too, have differentiated between private homosexual conduct (as in the *Morrison* case) and flaunted or widely publicized homosexuality (as in the case of a person whose rejection for a library position was upheld by the federal courts on this ground.[79]) Other courts have also stressed this factor, and have been far more sympathetic to the genuine privacy claim.

Do the position and its sensitivity affect the homosexual's rights?

Courts have said that an applicant for a sensitive position may be more vulnerable to blackmail, which is a feared effect of employing a homosexual. The relationship between the homosexual liaison and the job has also been stressed. In the *Morrison* case, for example, there had been no involvement of students or fellow teachers. In sharp contrast is a recent Wisconsin case upholding the discharge of a house parent at a state institution for mentally retarded teenaged boys.[80] He had freely discussed his homosexuality in front of his impressionable charges, and thus in the court's view jeopardized his highly sensitive and special role.

May a public employee forfeit protection by misrepresenting his or her homosexual involvement?

Yes, suggests one important federal court of appeals decision. The case involved a Maryland public school teacher who had been dismissed for being a homosexual. When he sought reinstatement, the court of appeals upheld his substantive claim, finding a constitutionally protected interest in private homosexual activity.[81] The court also held that the teacher could not be discharged because of public statements he had made after his removal, since these were within his freedom of expression. But the teacher ultimately lost because he had lied to school authorities about his homosexuality at the time of his initial employment.[82] Clearly there is a risk either way. If employees conceal their homosexuality, they may later be faced with the charge of lying; if, on the other hand, they make full disclosure when they seek a job, their applications may be rejected.

NOTES

1. *Bruns v. Pomerlau,* 319 F. Supp. 58 (D. Md. 1970).
2. *Cook v. Hudson,* 511 F.2d 744 (5th Cir. 1975), *cert. dismissed as improvidently granted,* 429 US. 165 (1976).
3. *Mindel v. Civil Service Commission,* 312 F. Supp. 485 (N.D. Cal. 1970); *Carter v. United States,* 407 F.2d 1238 (D.C. Cir. 1968); *New York Times,* April 4, 1969, p. 30, cols. 6–8.
4. *Montgomery County v. Walsh,* 274 Md. 489, 336 A.2d 97 (1975).
5. *Singer v. United States Civil Service Commission,* 530 F.2d 247 (9th Cir. 1976).
6. *Gayer v. Schlesinger,* 490 F.2d 740, 751 (D.C. Cir. 1973).
7. *Richardson v. Hampton,* 345 F. Supp. 600, 609 (D.D.C. 1972).
8. *Gayer v. Laird,* 332 F. Supp. 644, 169 (D.D.C. 1971).
9. *Scott v. Macy,* 402 F.2d 644, 648 (D.C. Cir. 1968).
10. *Anonymous v. Kissinger,* 499 F.2d 1097, 1102 (D.C. Cir. 1974).
11. 5 U.S.C. §§ 552 et seq. (1970).
12. 5 U.S.C. § 552 (1970).
13. 5 U.S.C. § 552A(G)(4) (1970).
14. *Carmel by the Sea v. Young,* 2 Cal. 3rd 259, 466 P.2d 225, 85 Cal Rptr. 1 (1970).
15. *Montgomery County v. Walsh,* 274 Md. 489, 336 A.2d 97 (1975); *Illinois State Employees Association v. Walker,* 57 Ill. 2d 512, 315 N.E.2d 9 (1974); *County of Nevada v. MacMillen,* 11 Cal. 3rd 662, 522 P.2d 1345, 114 Cal. Rptr. 345 (1974).
16. *O'Brien v. Jordan,* 544 F.2d 543 (1st Cir. 1976).
17. *California Bankers Association, v. Schultz,* 416 U.S. 21 (1974).
18. *Gardner v. Broderick,* 392 U.S. 273, 278 (1968).
19. *Slochower v. Board of Education,* 350 U.S. 551 (1956).
20. *Uniformed Sanitationmen's Association v. Commissioner of Sanitation,* 392 U.S. 280 (1968).
21. N.Y. Exec. Law 8296 (14) (Supp. 1977).
22. *New York Times,* April 18, 1976, p. 1, col. 4.
23. *Richardson v. Pasadena,* 500 S.W.2d 175 (Tex. App. 1973).
24. *Stape v. Civil Service Commission,* 404 Pa. 354, 172 A.2d 161 (1961); *Molino v. Board of Public Safety,* 154 Conn. 368, 225 A.2d 805 (1966).
25. *Seattle Police Officers Guild v. Seattle,* 80 Wash. 2d 307, 494 P.2d 485 (1970).

26. *Stape v. Civil Service Commission*, 404 Pa. 354, 172 A.2d 161 (1961); *Molino v. Board of Public Safety*, 154 Conn. 368, 225 A.2d 805 (1966).

27. *Powell v. Zuckert*, 366 F.2d 634 (D.C. Cir. 1966).

28. *Saylor v. United States*, 374 F.2d 894 (Ct. Cl. 1967).

29. *United States v. Donato*, 269 F. Supp. 921 (S.D.N.Y.), affirmed, 379 F.2d 863 (2d Cir. 1965).

30. *United States v. Blok*, 188 F.2d 1019 (D.C. Cir. 1951).

31. *White v. Davis*, 13 Cal. 3rd 757, 533 P. 2d 222, 120 Cal. Rptr. 94 (1975).

32. 319 F. Supp. 58 (D. Md. 1970).

33. *Doherty v. Wilson*, 356 F. Supp. 35 (M.D. Ga. 1973).

34. Ibid., p. 41.

35. *Battle v. Mulholland*, 439 F.2d 321 (5th Cir. 1971).

36. Ibid., p. 325.

37. *Cook v. Hudson*, 511 F.2d 744 (5th Cir. 1975), *cert. dismissed as improvidently granted*, 429 U.S. 165 (1976).

38. *Pierce v. Society of Sisters*, 268 U.S. 510 (1925).

39. *Berry v. Macon County Board of Education*, 380 F. Supp. 1244 (M.D. Ala. 1971).

40. *Cook v. Hudson*, 511 F.2d 744 (5th Cir. 1975).

41. *Cook v. Hudson*, 429 U.S. 165 (1976).

42. *Appeal of Drain*, 36 Ohio Misc. 157, 304 N.E.2d 257 (1970).

43. *Herzbrun v. Milwaukee County*, 338 F. Supp. 736, 738 (E.D. Wis. 1972).

44. 1 Cal. 3d 214, 461 P.2d 375, 82 Cal. Rptr. 175 (1969).

45. 1 Cal. 3d. at 229, 461 P.2d at 386, 82 Cal. Rptr. at 186.

46. See O'Neil, *The Private Lives of Public Employees*, 51 *Oregon Law Review* 70, 102–12 (1971).

47. *Zekas v. Baldwin*, 334 F. Supp. 1158 (E.D. Wis. 1970).

48. *Carter v. United States*, 407 F.2d 1238 (D.C. Cir. 1968).

49. Ibid, pp. 1246–1247.

50. *Muller v. Conlisk*, 429 F.2d 901 (7th Cir. 1970).

51. *Braxton v. Board of Public Instruction*, 303 F. Supp. 958 (M.D. Fla. 1969).

52. *Dwen v. Barry*, 483 F.2d 1126 (2d Cir. 1973).

53. 425 U.S. 238 (1976).

54. Ibid., p. 247.

55. Ibid., p. 248.

56. Ibid., p. 249.

57. Ibid., p. 254–56.

58. *Brown v. Schlesinger*, 365 F. Supp. 1204 (E.D. Va. 1973); *Garmon v. Walker*, 358 F. Supp. 206 (W.D.N.C. 1973).

59. *Earwood v. Continental Southeast Lines, Inc.*, 539 F.2d 1349, 1351 n.6 (4th Cir. 1976) (cases cited from other circuits).

60. *Slocum v. Fire and Police Commission of East Peoria*, 8 Ill. App. 2d 465, 290 N.E.2d 28 (1972).
61. *Matter of Heather Martin*, No. 8156 (N.Y. Comm'r of Educ. August 31, 1971).
62. *In re School District of Kingsley and Kingsley Board of Education Association*, 56 Lab. Arb. 1138 (1971).
63. *Tardif v. Quinn*, 545 F.2d 761 (1st Cir. 1976).
64. *East Hartford Education Association v. Board of Education of East Hartford*, 562 F.2d 838 (2d Cir. 1977).
65. *Carter v. United States*, 407 F.2d 1238 (D.C. Cir. 1968).
66. *Board of Trustees v. Stubblefield*, 16 Cal. App. 3rd 820, 94 Cal. Rptr. 318 (1971).
67. *Sedule v. Capital School District*, 425 F. Supp. 552 (D.Del. 1976); *Hollenbaugh v. Carnegie Free Library*, 436 F. Supp. 1328 (W.D. Pa. 1977).
68. *Pettit v. State Board of Education*, 10 Cal. 3rd 29, 513 P.2d 889, 109 Cal. Rptr. 665 (1973).
69. 10 Cal. 3rd at 35, 513 P.2d at 893, 109 Cal. Rptr. at 669.
70. *Andrews v. Drew Municipal Separate School District*, 507 F.2d 611 (5th Cir. 1975).
71. *Montoya v. Taos Municipal School District*, No. 76-557 (D.N.M. April 14, 1977), 11 Clearinghouse Review 145
72. *In re Grossman*, 316 A.2d 39 (N.J. 1974); *Grossman v. Bernards Township Board of Education*, 538 F.2d 319 (3d Cir.), *cert. denied*, 429 U.S. 897 (1976).
73. *Morrison v. State Board of Education*, 1 Cal. 3rd 214, 461 P.2d 375, 82 Cal. Rptr. 175 (1969); *Norton v. Macy*, 417 F.2d 1161 (D.C. Cir. 1969).
74. *Board of Education of Long Beach Unified School District, v. M.*, 566 P.2d 602 (Cal. 1977).
75. *Doe v. Commonwealth's Attorney*, 425 U.S. 901 (1976).
76. *Singer v. Civil Service Commission*, 429 U.S. 1034 (1977).
77. *Gaylord v. Tacoma School District No. 10*, 88 Wash. 2d 286, 559 P.2d 1340 (1976) *cert. denied*, 98 S. Ct. 234 (1977).
78. *44 United States Law Week* (July 15, 1975).
79. *McConnell v. Anderson*, 451 F.2d 193 (8th Cir. 1971).
80. *Safransky v. State Personnel Board*, 62 Wis. 464, 215 N.W.2d 379 (1974).
81. *Acanfora v. Board of Education*, 491 F.2d 498 (4th Cir. 1974).
82. Ibid., p. 504.

VI

Race and Sex Discrimination

Few areas of the law have expanded faster in the last decade than the area dealing with redress of race and sex discrimination. Both minority groups and women have taken their claims to the courts and to federal and state agencies in record numbers. The principal cause of the recent rise in antidiscrimination activity is the enactment of the Civil Rights Act of 1964. Title VII of that law forbids discrimination in employment.[1] Originally, the law was limited to private employers and their employees, but in 1972 was extended to include the public sector as well. Since that time, the volume of litigation against government agencies has grown as rapidly as the number of suits against private employers grew during the 1960s. The purpose of this chapter is to analyze not only Title VII but several other laws aiding the public employee who feels that he or she has been discriminated against because of race or sex. We will also explore the available remedies, including such sensitive issues as the propriety of quota hiring orders.

RACIAL DISCRIMINATION

What laws protect public employees from race discrimination?

It has long been clear that government may not discriminate against its employees or applicants on the basis of race. Less clear, until quite recently, were the remedies available to redress such discrimination. Roughly two-thirds of the states have enacted fair employment practices or antidiscrimination laws, most of which cover state and local as well as private employment. Many cities also have such laws to supplement state statutes.

The major concern of this chapter, however, is with the protections afforded by federal law. Three statutes are especially pertinent. In 1866, Congress enacted a law, often referred to as section 1981, that grants to all people the same right to make and enforce contracts as is enjoyed by white citizens.[2] This law, designed to enhance the rights of former slaves after the Civil War, has been held to cover employment, since a job clearly involves a "contract." Another post-Civil War law, section 1983, gives a federal remedy to any person who has been deprived of his or her civil rights by any other person "acting under color of state law."[3] Since a state or local government agency clearly "acts under color of state law," this provision also protects victims of employment discrimination.

The third, most recent, and now most important provision is Title VII of the Civil Rights Act of 1964.[4] That law forbids discrimination in employment on the basis of race, color, religion, or national origin. Originally, Title VII applied to private employers only and not to the government. In 1972, Congress added section 717, which extends the full protections of Title VII to persons discriminated against by federal government agencies.[5]

This amendment left open the question of whether federal employees could invoke the other laws—sections 1981 and 1983—as could persons in other sectors. In summer 1976, the Supreme Court settled the issue, holding that Congress had meant section 717 to provide the *exclusive* remedy for persons complaining of federal employment discrimination.[6] Thus sections 1981 and 1983 remain available to state and local employees and job applicants, but not to those alleging bias on the part of the federal government.

When Congress enacted Title VII, it created the Equal Employment Opportunity Commission (EEOC) to enforce the new law.[7] This agency has responsibility for investigating complaints of discrimination, and trying to settle them informally. It cannot compel anyone to do anything, and provides only a preliminary stage in a process that will be described more fully later.

Who is protected by these laws?

Although the post-Civil War laws were designed to protect the rights of blacks (former slaves), they were later extended to other racial minority groups—Chicanos, Puerto Ricans, Asians, Filipinos, American Indians—who may be the victims of discrimination. Title VII is available to all racial minority groups.[8] Employment discrimination claims increasingly involve nonblack plaintiffs.

Are whites protected against government employment discrimination?

In the abstract, there has been little doubt that race discrimination was as unlawful against whites as against minorities. But there was uncertainty about the availability of remedies until the Supreme Court held in 1976 that the basic federal antidiscrimination laws were available equally to whites and blacks.[9] The purpose of Title VII, said the Court, was to forbid all forms of racial discrimination, and that included discrimination against whites. The post-Civil War laws, although originally enacted for the benefit of blacks, were equally available to others—even though section 1983 gave to others the same rights "as [are] enjoyed by white persons." The Court found that the intent of Congress had been not to differentiate by color among persons seeking relief against discrimination.

What forms of employment discrimination are prohibited?

These laws clearly forbid, but are not limited to, the refusal to hire an applicant because of race. Failure to promote qualified persons because of race, or to consider them on an equal footing for promotion is also unlawful. Unequal compensation or salary levels are also in violation of these laws. Discrimination in initial hiring may take many forms, such as the use of certain educational or experience requirements that treat minority applicants unfairly, and the use of biased tests or examinations. These and other practices may be just as unlawful as the outright refusal to consider a person because of his or her race, and are probably more pervasive. Discrimination comes in many forms, subtle or complex as well as simple and obvious. (In a later section, we will consider in some detail what must be proved to establish a case of unlawful discrimination.)

What procedure should a victim of federal employment discrimination follow?

A person who feels he or she has been the victim of federal employment discrimination should first contact the Equal Employment Opportunity counselor in the agency where the discrimination occurred.[10] If the counselor cannot bring about a satisfactory adjustment, the complainant may then seek an administrative hearing before a Civil Service examiner. The examiner will make a recommendation to the head of the agency, based upon the facts developed at the hearing and an independent examination of the complaint. The agency head then makes a decision, of which the complainant is informed. If the complainant wishes not to accept this decision, there are two alternatives: (1) proceed to the federal district court, or (2) appeal to the Civil Service Commission Board of Appeals and Review. If the person takes the second alternative—going to the Civil Service Commission, and the commission rejects the claim, a suit may be filed in a federal court. Finally, the employee may go to court if within a specified period the agency head or the Civil Service Commission has failed to take any action on the complaint.

What happens in the federal court after a complaint has been heard within the agency or the Civil Service Commission?

Some government agencies have argued that the court should review the record, rather than taking testimony, treating the suit as an appeal from a federal agency proceeding. Several lower federal courts have agreed. But the Supreme Court recently held that federal employees, like others pursuing claims under Title VII, were entitled to a full hearing in the federal district court—a "trial de novo"—even though they had already had a hearing within the agency.[11] While this might give federal employees "two strings to the bow," that was what Congress intended.

What procedure should a victim of state or local employment discrimination follow?

In order to invoke the old Civil Rights Laws (sections 1981 and 1983), an aggrieved person need only file a suit in the federal district court. If, however, the person wishes to seek remedies provided by Title VII, the procedure is rather complex and includes these steps:

1. In a state that does not have its own antidiscrimination laws and/or agency, the employee must file a complaint with the Equal Employment Opportunity Commission within 180 days of the discriminatory act.

2. In a state that does have its own antidiscrimination laws, the state agency must be given 60 days to resolve the issue before federal relief is sought. The complainant may go to the EEOC only after that time. Even if a charge has been filed with the state or local agency, the complainant must protect the eventual right to federal recourse. This is done by filing with the EEOC within 300 days of the discriminatory act, or within 30 days after receiving notice that the state or local agency has dropped the case, whichever comes first.

3. A "right-to-sue letter" must be obtained by the complainant from the EEOC before he or she can bring suit in federal court under Title VII. Such a letter may be obtained as a matter of right any time after the complaint has been before the EEOC for 180 days, regardless of whether the commission has taken any action. A letter may be demanded if neither the state/local agency nor the EEOC has taken any action on the complaint.

4. After receiving the right-to-sue letter, the complainant must file suit in the federal district court within 90 days, or will thereafter be barred from suing.

Because of this complex interaction of systems, the wisest procedure is to file state and federal charges at the same time. A charge filed with the EEOC should be accompanied by a letter noting that similar charges have been filed with the state or local agency and asking that the EEOC take over the case after 60 days—the time by which the state or local agency's primary control of the complaint will lapse.

Two additional factors affect the decision of whether or not to seek a right-to-sue letter. Rarely will the EEOC be able to complete action on a complaint within 180 days. If there is reason to proceed without delay, the case should be taken to court immediately rather than waiting for the EEOC to process the complaint. Many charges of discrimination raise factual questions requiring extensive investigation before court action can occur. Under Title VII, the EEOC is to investigate complaints as part of its pretrial conciliation efforts. Leaving the pretrial investigation and discovery to the commission may therefore save money, even though the complainant loses some degree of control over the fact-finding process.

In order to facilitate redress of discrimination, Congress provided in Title VII that the federal courts may appoint an attorney for the complainant and may also authorize the filing of a suit without payment of court costs or fees, or the posting of a bond or other security that would be required in a typical suit over employment. Thus the burdens and costs of pursuing these remedies are further reduced in appropriate cases. The Supreme Court has recently held that in extenuating circumstances, especially those resulting from the heavy backlog of cases pending in the EEOC, the time limit for filing suit may be relaxed, if necessary, to achieve fairness.[12]

What must a complainant prove in a discrimination case?

At the start, the complainant must establish at least the following elements: (1) that he or she belongs to a minority group, (2) that he or she applied for the job and was qualified for it, (3) that despite these qualifications, he or she was denied the job (or was passed over for a promotion); and (4) that after the rejection, the employer continued to seek applications from people with the complainant's qualifications.[13] Such proof will establish what lawyers call a "prima facie case" and will usually shift the burden of proof to the employer.

Far more common (and usually more effective) than individual employee complaints are suits on behalf of groups (classes) of employees or applicants that allege that a particular practice of an employer discriminates against members of the group seeking employment or advancement. Thus it may be claimed that a high school diploma requirement discriminates against blacks. Or a standardized test given to all applicants (in English) may be alleged to discriminate against persons of Spanish-speaking backgrounds. Or a uniform height minimum rule may be challenged as discriminatory against Asians. Many cases have considered such class actions and the validity of practices of public as well as private employers.

The Supreme Court has announced a general approach governing such suits. In the 1971 case of *Griggs v. Duke Power Co.*,[14] the Court considered the validity of a private employer's testing procedures and educational requirements. It had been shown that whites scored far better on the test than blacks, and that a far higher percentage of white than black applicants possessed the required high school diploma. "If," said the Supreme Court, "an employment practice which operates to exclude Negroes cannot be shown to be related to job performance, the practice is prohibited." The Court clearly rejected the argument that a discriminatory *intent* or *purpose* must be shown; it was enough that the *effect* be to exclude disproportionate numbers of minority applicants. Moreover, the Court insisted that job qualifications could not be measured solely by formal requirements: "Diplomas and tests are useful servants, but Congress has mandated the commonsense proposition that they are not to become masters of reality."[15]

Since the *Griggs* decision, many lower courts have applied this formula to public employment. Where a particular educational or experience requirement or test is shown to exclude disproportionate numbers of minority applicants, the agency must "validate" that requirement since (in the words of the *Griggs* opinion) "Congress has placed on the employer the burden of showing that any given requirement must have a manifest relationship to the employment in question."[16] If the employer fails to prove its validity, the practice or procedure will be set aside.

A 1976 Supreme Court decision has raised new
questions in this area. The case involved a challenge by
black applicants for the District of Columbia police
force. They claimed that testing procedures used by the
department unconstitutionally discriminated against minorities because they excluded disproportionate numbers of black applicants. (The suit was based on the
Constitution because it was brought before the 1972
amendments made Title VII applicable to public employment.) The court of appeals followed the *Griggs*
analysis and held the tests invalid.[17] The Supreme
Court, however, took a different view: Since the suit
rested on the Constitution and not on Title VII, mere
proof of racially disproportionate effect was not
enough; there must also be some proof of racially
discriminatory purpose or intent in order to set aside
testing procedures of a government agency.[18] The
Court did specifically point out that this was not a Title
VII case, and that the standard to be applied under the
Constitution was lower, but the case does suggest that
the Supreme Court may at some time qualify the formula announced in *Griggs*.

How may an employer respond to such a suit?

Title VII offers several possible defenses to a charge
of employment discrimination. First, a negative personnel decision may be shown to be based upon a bona
fide seniority or merit system—that is, a system that is
free of racial discrimination. (Several recent cases have
involved the conflict between equal employment opportunity and seniority systems in the private sector, but
the issue has not yet been adjudicated in government
employment.[19])

Second and more important, the agency may demonstrate the validity of the requirement or test alleged to
be discriminatory. Validation is a rather complex
process, to which the courts have recently devoted
much attention. Federal agencies, especially the Equal
Employment Opportunity Commission, have been

drafting regulations for the validation of employment tests, but final rules have not yet been approved. The basic question of validity, as the courts define it, is whether "the disproportionate impact was simply the result of a proper test demonstrating the lesser ability of [minority] candidates to perform the job satisfactorily."[20] If that correlation cannot be shown, the test is invalid. Validation can proceed in different ways— through *construct* validation (identifying physical, mental, and psychological traits required on the job, and then designing a test to determine the presence of those traits); or *content* validation (matching the specific skills and aptitudes required by the job with those evaluated by the test or other requirement.[21] Courts have not insisted that a particular kind of validation be used, so long as the process ensures the necessary correlation between the test or requirement and the job performance. Under this formula, a number of government job conditions have been found invalid—minimum height and weight requirements for police and fire positions;[22] current events and mathematics questions on tests for manual labor jobs;[23] and other physical and mental tests of vaious types.[24]

In this area, too, the Supreme Court's recent *Davis* (D.C. Police) case may have raised some doubts. Most of the opinion dealt with the constitutional standards, and avoided Title VII issues. But the Court did comment in passing about the validation procedures used under Title VII. The district court had held the challenged tests to be valid because there was a correlation between performance on them and the requirements of the police training program.[25] The court of appeals disagreed, since the evidence showed only that applicants would perform about the same on a later written test as on an earlier examination, and not (as *Griggs* seemed to require) that the written tests correlated with the actual needs of the job.[26] Moreover, the court of appeals was troubled because all applicants who scored below a certain level on the initial examination were excluded from the training program, so that even the correlation between the two sets of tests was incomplete.[27] But the Supreme Court agreed with the district court that the initial tests could be validated by their relationship to performance in the training program. This, said the Court with a reference back to *Griggs,* "seems to us the much more sensible construction of the job relatedness requirement."[28] The decision is, however, confusing since the Title VII issue was really not before the Court and since there was in the case at least one validation study to which the Supreme Court gave greater weight than had the court of appeals. Finally, the Supreme Court noted that the training program was still undergoing modification and that a later suit could still "challenge any deficiencies in the recruiting practices under prevailing Title VII standards."[29]

If employment discrimination is proved, what remedies are available?

In general, the remedies are of four types: (1) an order to hire, reinstate, or promote the employee or employes against whom discrimination has been practiced; (2) an injunction against the repetition or continuation of the practice found to be discriminatory; (3) an award of back pay or actual wages that the victims of discrimination would have earned had the discrimination not been practiced; and (4) in extraordinary cases, an award of punitive damages against an employer found to have discriminated in bad faith.

May back pay be recovered from a state or local government?

In early Title VII cases, courts refused to enter back pay awards against state and local governments, since the Eleventh Amendment to the Constitution forbids suits against states. But the Supreme Court held in 1976 that the "sovereign immunity" of states does not protect them against back pay orders.[30] The legislation authorizing remedies against discrimination rested on the provisions of the Fourteenth Amendment. This later amendment allowed Congress to authorize relief, even against state and local governments, where necessary to redress racial discrimination. Thus suits to recover money from states, which might be barred in other settings, were proper here.

The scope of the back-pay provisions is rather broad. The purposes of such an award are to put the employee where he or she would have been without the discrimination, and to deter future violations. The Supreme Court held in 1975 that a complainant need not show bad faith or a discriminatory purpose in order to recover back pay; the agency head's state of mind is irrelevant for back-pay purposes.[31]

May a public employee recover punitive damages for race discrimination?

Some courts have found authority to award damages going beyond simple back pay under sections 1981 and 1983. Such claims run against the individual agency head or other person who made the discriminatory decision, and not against the agency or government itself; the remedy is based on a personal denial of civil rights by one person against another. Less probable is the availability of punitive damages under Title VII. The language of the statute does not authorize such relief, and most courts have held that damages beyond back pay are not available.[32]

May a court require quota hiring to remedy past discrimination?

Yes. A number of courts have ordered a state or local agency to hire a specified percentage of minority applicants—one black for every three positions filled, for example—in order to remedy the effects of past racial discrimination. Without specific statutory language, these courts have found an implied basis for such orders in the older civil rights statutes and even in Title VII.[33] However, the conditions are rather limited: First, there must be a history of discrimination against a minority group, or statistical evidence showing a strong pattern of exclusion. Second, people to be included within the quota must be qualified for the job. Third, the order is almost always limited to a specific time period (though it may be renewed if the result has not been accomplished within that period). And fourth, there is almost always a finding that less drastic forms of relief would not suffice. Sometimes a court will also consider the number of persons belonging to the preferred group in the area or region affected by the order.[34]

There are increasing qualifications, however. One federal court declined to decree quota hiring because the potential of less drastic means had not been exhausted, and the New Jersey Supreme Court set aside the quota-hiring order of an administrative agency on both constitutional and statutory grounds.[35] There are several reasons for the reluctance to order or sustain racial quotas. One is the provision of Title VII, section 703 (j), that this law shall not be interpreted to require an employer "to grant preferential treatment to any individual or group on account of any imbalance which may exist with respect to the total number or percentage of persons of any race, color . . . in comparison with the total number or percentage of persons of such race, color . . . in any community . . . or in the available work force."[36] At least one court has found this language inapplicable to the results of past discriminatory practices, though others have been deterred by it from quota-hiring orders in Title VII cases. Elsewhere courts have drawn a distinction between initial hiring and promotion for purpose of relief. Requiring that a percentage of minority applicants be accepted into the work force seems less drastic than applying a similar quota to the promotion of persons of different races already in the work force. In the promotion case, some current employees, "regardless of their qualifications and standing in competitive examinations . . . may be bypassed for advancement solely because they are white."[37]

be justified in terms of the peculiar requirements of the particular job and not on the basis of a general principle such as the desirability of spreading work.[48]

Under these guidelines, it is clear that a merely traditional, historic, or esthetic rationale would not pass muster. Nor would the preferences of co-workers or of customers justify a gender-based distinction. Thus it has been held that sex is not a bona fide qualification for the position of airline flight attendant, and male stewards have been hired in substantial numbers.[49] A narrow qualification has recently been recognized, however, to the limited scope of the BFOQ. One federal district court has held that an airline may require stewardesses to discontinue flying upon learning that they are pregnant, but solely for compelling safety considerations.[50] Otherwise, the exception is a narrow one indeed, and in no sense undermines the basic purposes of Title VII's guarantee of equality of access to employment regardless of sex.

The most recent and clearest pronouncement of the Supreme Court on this subject has already been cited in Chapter II, but bears attention here as well. In *Dothard v. Rawlinson*,[51] the Court held in June 1977 that Alabama's height and weight requirements for prison guards violated Title VII because they excluded 40% of women but only 1% of men. The Court noted that the state had failed to demonstrate the necessity of a certain physical size to the performance of routine guard duties, and that male sex was clearly not a bona fide occupational qualification. The scope of this ruling was clarified by the companion judgment that Alabama could employ only men for sometimes violent "contact" duty in maximum security all-male prisons. In this very limited situation, the Court acknowledged that male sex was a bona fide occupational qualification and thus survived the rigorous review of Title VII.

Are laws designed to "protect" women in employment still valid?

In most cases, they are not. Over the years, and sometimes for the best of motives, state legislatures enacted laws restricting the hours that women may work, the amount of weight they may lift, the types of jobs to which they may be assigned, and other conditions of employment. Many such laws have recently been challenged and have been held either unconstitutional or in violation of federal or state laws forbidding sex discrimination.[52] The EEOC guidelines do not regard such laws as justifying otherwise invalid sex differentiation, or even as evidence of a BFOQ.[53] The EEOC has held, for example, that sex is not a valid qualification for occupations involving more than ten hours work per day where sex would not justify distinctions in that job during shorter work periods. Similar results have been reached with regard to "protective" laws limiting the weight that women could lift or carry, or barring certain "dangerous" or "unladylike" occupations to women. In order to meet the BFOQ test, any such laws must be shown to rest on a business necessity inherent in the position.

What of laws that forbid the employment of both spouses in the same agency or department?

Many government agencies have rules against "nepotism"—that is, against employing husband and wife (or parent and child, and sometimes more distant relatives) in the same agency. Such laws are designed to avoid placing one member of the family in a position that may unfairly favor relatives as against other persons in the agency. But such rules have often been applied to situations in which two spouses are simply fellow employees and neither has any control or direction over the other. Some such rules are by their terms discriminatory against women—because they require the wife to resign, for example, wherever nepotism exists. Even where the terms of the rule are neutral, it may have a discriminatory effect (if, for example, it disproportionately reaches members of one sex). In such a case, the rule would appear to be in violation of Title VII unless it could be justified under the BFOQ standards by reason of "business necessity."

One federal court of appeals decision has upheld an antinepotism rule challenged under section 1983.[54] Although the terms of the rule prohibited a husband-wife combination from teaching in the same school, the facts of the case involved an administrator-teacher relationship that did pose a risk of conflict of interest. Moreover, the husband was discharged when the violation of the rule came to light. Because of the small size of the school district, there was apparently no alternative (such as the transfer of one spouse) by which to avoid the potential conflict. This decision leaves open the question of how broader antinepotism rules would fare under Title VII as well as under section 1983.

Do mandatory maternity-leave policies constitute unlawful sex discrimination?

Yes, if they do not provide for individualized determinations. In 1974, the Supreme Court held unconstitutional the maternity leave policies of several school boards that required teachers to take leave five months before the anticipated birth of a child, and barred them from returning to work for a similar period after delivery.[55] Such policies were justified by the need to keep unfit teachers out of the classroom, and to maintain continuity of instruction. But the Court found both interests poorly served by such policies. Some teachers were quite fit to continue teaching well after the fifth month; the board's legitimate interest in physical fitness could be well served by judging the individual capacity of each pregnant teacher. As for continuity of instruction, the challenged policy actually thwarted school needs; the required leave date might fall in the middle of a term or even in mid-week. A more flexible policy would not only better meet the teacher's needs, but would permit the completion of an instructional period and allow an orderly transition. Much the same could be said of policies governing the teacher's return to the classroom following delivery of the child: Some teachers might be able to resume their duties after one month while others might not be ready even at five months—again, the matter was best determined by judging individual qualifications rather than by arbitrary and rigid rules.

There are other employment disabilities caused by maternity and pregnancy. Their status is in some doubt as the result of recent regulations and decisions. The Equal Employment Opportunity Commission issued regulations requiring that pregnancy be treated like other disabilities, covered by appropriate insurance, eligible for cumulative use of sick-leave time, etc.[56] The Supreme Court held in December 1976, however, that these regulations conflict with Title VII and are therefore invalid.[57] Thus employer plans that excluded pregnancy from disability coverage are now valid under Title VII. Barely two weeks later, the New York Court of Appeals ruled that under the state Human Rights Law employers must pay benefits to women employees who miss work because of pregnancy.[58] Although the New York court recognized the conflict with the U.S. Supreme Court, federal law does not preclude a state from going further in protecting women's rights. The answer to many of these questions may now depend upon whether other states follow New York or adhere to the federal Supreme Court standard.

What procedure should a public employee follow in a case of alleged sex discrimination?

For a federal employee, the procedure under Title VII is the same as that described earlier for claims of racial discrimination. This procedure involves appeal within the agency, after which the employee may go to the Civil Service Commission and eventually to the courts. For state and local employees, the procedure under Title VII is more complex, as described for racial discrimination claims on pages 129–131. State and local government employees may also go directly to court if they wish to file suit against the agency head under section 1983.

Under the Equal Pay Act, an employee claiming discrimination should contact a local office of the Wage and Hour Division of the U.S. Department of Labor, which has responsibility for enforcing this law. The department will typically investigate, protecting the anonymity of the complainant. If it finds discrimination, it will bring suit against the employer. Alternatively, the individual may bring suit directly against the employer without going to the Labor Department. Such a suit must be brought within two years (or within three years if the discrimination is "willful").

What must an employee prove under a sex discrimination charge?

As in a racial discrimination case, the employee charging sex discrimination in hiring or promotion must establish that he or she was qualified for the position, that despite these qualifications the application was rejected, and that the agency thereafter continued to seek applicants with similar qualifications. Proof of a disproportionate effect upon women (or men) will shift the burden of proof to the employer. For example, in several recent cases, women have shown that height and weight minimums serve to exclude virtually all otherwise qualified women from fire, police, and other municipal services.[59] When such an effect is shown, the agency must demonstrate the validity of the rules in much the same way as in the racial discrimination context. If it can be shown that a certain height or weight is essential to the performance of the job, that may validate the condition. No employment criterion with a disproportionate impact against women has yet been upheld under Title VII. (Since such requirements do not differentiate explicitly on the basis of sex as such, the BFOQ analysis is not relevant here, although the process of validation may be rather similar.)

Under the Equal Pay Act, a complainant must prove that men and women receiving different pay levels work in the same establishment—that is, in the same physical location or facility. The jobs involved must require equal skill, effort, and responsibility (each element to be examined separately). The work must be performed under similar working conditions. Finally, the tasks themselves must be substantially similar, even if not identical, to support a claim that disparate pay scales violate the law. If any one of these tests is not met, the employer cannot be held to have violated the Equal Pay Act—although the employer may not avoid an otherwise valid claim by reducing male compensation levels to create an artificial parity.

What remedies are available when unlawful sex discrimination has been proved?

As with race discrimination, a successful complainant will be entitled to be hired, rehired, or promoted and thus put where he or she would have been if not for the unlawful discrimination. An injunction may also be issued, forbidding the repetition or continuation of an unlawful policy or practice. The remedy of back pay is also available to offset the effects of discrimination. Under Title VII, back pay may be recovered for two years prior to the filing of a claim with the EEOC or a suit in court. Under the Equal Pay Act, the normal limit on back pay is also two years. A court may, however, award back pay for a period up to three years if it finds the employer's violation to have been "willful." Under section 1983, the only limit on back pay as a possible remedy is the judge's discretion. As with racial discrimination, two very recent Supreme Court decisions concerning back pay under Title VII are relevant here: one holding that an employer's good faith is no defense to a back-pay claim,[60] and the other holding that federal courts may award back pay against state and local governments despite the Eleventh Amendment barrier to suits against states.[61] Another recent federal law—Title IX of the Education Amendments of 1972—could provide a private remedy for persons in educational programs who have suffered sex discrimination; the one court of appeals to pass on the issue has, however, held that congress did not mean to allow recovery of damages under this law.[62]

May quota hiring be ordered in sex discrimination cases?

Yes, although such orders are much less frequent than in cases of racial discrimination. If a court finds that there has been a pattern of discrimination against either sex, and that less drastic measures would not suffice, it may order that a certain percentage of new employees be drawn from the disadvantaged sex. Such an order would undoubtedly be for a limited time, and would be dissolved when the desired goal had been achieved.[63] On the other hand, additional safeguards may be required to implement such a decree. Thus one court has recently issued an order preventing the layoff by a public agency of women recently hired under an affirmative action program; otherwise the normal operation of the seniority system would largely defeat the recent gains.[64]

May government agencies favor women in their hiring policies?

The status of preferential policies is less clear in regard to sex than to race. Where there has been a background of discrimination against women, and where a court might require preferential hiring, a voluntary preference would seem valid. It is also true that government agencies and those receiving government funds are required to adopt affirmative action programs for recruitment and consideration of women as well as minorities. Yet the case for preference for women rests on somewhat different premises; while women have been the victims of both overt and subtle discrimination, there is no evidence, for example, that women score less well than men on standardized tests. There is relatively little litigation on this issue, although the race-preference problem has now received much attention from the courts. One recent case at least touches upon the sex-preference question. A federal district court held that a state university had improperly given preference to women in recruitment for faculty positions. Although the university argued that it was bound by federal law to adopt an affirmative action program, the court ruled that it could not lawfully "predicate hiring and promotion decisions on gender-based criteria."[65] Moreover, "where sex is the sole factor upon which differential treatment is determined, there is no Constitutional justification for treating the sexes differently."[66] The scope of the decision may, however, be limited by the fact that the university apparently declined even to interview any of the 328 male applicants for the position in question, but hired 2 of the 57 women who applied.

The legality of sex-based preferential hiring policies is thus in some doubt. Special efforts to recruit women, and special attention to their candidacy, may be one thing; a refusal even to interview all male applicants may be quite another. It would be surprising if government agencies were forbidden by one law to do what another law requires them to do. The line between the two options may be a narrow and sometimes indistinct one, but government employers must increasingly follow that narrow path between discrimination *against* men, and preference *for* women (or vice versa).

What considerations govern the choice of a remedy?

By way of review, we might assess the factors that bear upon a sex discrimination victim's choice of a remedy. There are three possible options, the advantages and disadvantages of which should be carefully weighed:[67]

SECTION 1983
Advantages

1. All state and local public employees are covered (though federal employees may no longer use it).
2. It avoids both procedural delay and time requirements of Title VII.
3. Both sex and race discrimination are covered.
4. Back-pay awards are not limited in time, and punitive damages may be awarded.

Disadvantages

1. Only public officials (e.g., agency heads) are proper defendants, and they enjoy immunity from money damages when acting in good faith.
2. No investigation or conciliation effort is assured before trial.
3. The standard of review may be much less advantageous.
4. Preferential or extraordinary remedies are available only where a history of intentional discrimination is proved.

TITLE VII
Advantages

1. EEOC investigation and conciliation efforts are conducted at no expense to complainant.
2. EEOC may actually litigate the claim in a proper case.
3. Extraordinary remedies such as retroactive seniority may be ordered.
4. Attorneys' fees and other costs may be recovered.
5. Federal courts are required to expedite such suits and may appoint attorneys for the complainant.

Disadvantages

1. Time-consuming procedures must be exhausted.
2. Two-year time limit is imposed on recovery of back pay.
3. Not all public employees are covered.

EQUAL PAY ACT
Advantages
1. Secretary of Labor is charged with enforcement.
2. Criminal penalties may be imposed on willful violators.
3. Attorneys' fees and court costs are recoverable.
4. Penalties are recoverable up to the amount of back pay awarded, within the court's discretion.

Disadvantages
1. Not all public employees are covered.
2. Public enforcement procedure may be time-consuming.
3. It reaches claims of sex discrimination only.

NOTES

1. 42 U.S.C. § 2000e (1970).
2. 42 U.S.C. § 1981 (1970).
3. 42 U.S.C. § 1983 (1970).
4. 42 U.S.C. § 2000e (1970).
5. 42 U.S.C. § 2000e-16 (1970).
6. *Brown v. General Services Administration,* 425 U.S. 820 (1976).
7. 42 U.S.C. § 2000e-4 (1970).
8. *Chicano Police Officers Association v. Stoner,* 526 F.2d 431 (10th Cir. 1975).
9. *McDonald v. Santa Fe Trail Transportation Co.,* 427 U.S. 273 (1976).
10. 42 U.S.C. § 2000e-5 (1970).
11. *Chandler v. Roudebush,* 425 U.S. 840 (1976).
12. *Occidental Life Insurance Co. of Calif. v. Equal Employment Opportunity Commission.* 432 U.S. — (1977).
13. *Vulcan Society of New York City Fire Department, Inc. v. Civil Service Commission,* 490 F.2d 387 (2d Cir. 1973); *Jackson v. City of Akron,* 411 F. Supp. 680 (N.D. Ohio 1976).
14. 401 U.S. 424 (1971).
15. Ibid., p. 433.
16. *Castro v. Beecher,* 459 F.2d 725, 732 (1st Cir. 1972); *Bridgeport Guardians, Inc. v. Members of Bridgeport Civil Service Commission,* 482 F.2d 1333 (2d Cir. 1973).
17. *Davis v. Washington,* 512 F.2d 956 (D.C. Cir. 1975).
18. *Washington v. Davis,* 426 U.S. 229 (1976).
19. *Jersey Central Power & Light Co. v. Local Unions 327 et*

al., 508 F.2d 687 (3rd Cir. 1975); *Koch v. Yunich,* 533 F.2d 80 (2d Cir. 1976).

20. *Vulcan Society of New York City Fire Department, Inc. v. Civil Service Commission,* 490 F.2d 387, 392 (2d Cir. 1973).
21. *Bridgeport Guardians, Inc. v. Members of Bridgeport Civil Service Commission,* 482 F.2d 1333, 1337–38 (2d Cir. 1973).
22. *Mieth v. Dothard,* 418 F. Supp. 1169 (M.D. Ala. 1976).
23. *Vulcan Society of New York City Fire Department, Inc. v. Civil Service Commission,* 490 F.2d 387, 393–94 (2d Cir. 1973).
24. *Georgia Association of Educators v. Nix,* 407 F. Supp. 1102 (N.D. Ga. 1976).
25. *Davis v. Washington,* 348 F. Supp. 15 (D.D.C. 1972).
26. *Davis v. Washington,* 512 F.2d 956, 961–62 (D.C. Cir. 1975).
27. Ibid., pp. 963–64.
28. *Washington v. Davis,* 426 U.S. 229, 251 (1976).
29. Ibid., p. 252.
30. *Fitzpatrick v. Bitzer,* 427 U.S. 445 (1976).
31. *Albemarle Paper Co. v. Moody,* 422 U.S. 405 (1975).
32. *Howard v. Lockheed-Georgia Co.,* 372 F. Supp. 854 (N.D. Ga. 1974); *Loo v. Gerange,* 374 F. Supp. 1338 (D. Haw. 1974).
33. *Castro v. Beecher,* 459 F.2d 725 (1st Cir. 1972); *Carter v. Gallagher,* 452 F.2d 315 (8th Cir. 1972); *Morrow v. Crisler,* 491 F.2d 1053 (5th Cir. 1974); *Pennsylvania v. O'Neill,* 348 F. Supp. 1084 (E.D. Pa. 1972), *affirmed,* 473 F.2d 1029 (3rd Cir. 1973).
34. *Contractors Association of Eastern Pennsylvania v. Secretary of Labor,* 442 F.2d 159 (3rd Cir. 1971).
35. *Chance v. Board of Examiners,* 534 F. 2d 993, 998 (2d Cir. 1976).
36. 42 U.S.C. § 2000e-2(j) (1970).
37. *Kirkland v. New York State Department of Correctional Services,* 520 F.2d 420, 429 (2d Cir. 1975); *Lige v. Town of Montclair,* 72 N.J., 5,367 A.2d 833 (1976).
38. *International Brotherhood of Teamsters v. United States,* 431 U.S. 324 (1977).
39. Revised Order 4, 41 C.F.R. part 60-1 et seq.
40. *Reeves v. Eaves,* 411 F. Supp. 531 (N.D. Ga. 1976).
41. *Germann v. Kipp,* 429 F. Supp. 1323 (W.D. Mo. 1977).
42. 42 U.S.C. § 2000e-2(e) (1970).
43. 29 U.S.C. §§ 201 et seq. (1970).
44. *Cleveland Board of Education v. LaFleur,* 414 U.S. 632 (1974).
45. *General Electric Co. v. Gilbert,* 429 U.S. 125 (1976);

Geduldig v. Aiello, 417 U.S. 484 (1974); *Frontiero v. Richardson*, 411 U.S. 677 (1973); *Reed v. Reed*, 404 U.S. 71 (1971).

46. *Craig v. Boren*, 429 U.S. 190 (1976).

47. *Sail'er Inn, Inc. v. Kirby*, 5 Cal. 3rd 1, 485 P.2d 529, 95 Cal. Rptr. 329 (1971).

48. *Rosenfeld v. Southern Pacific Co.*, 444 F.2d 1219 (9th Cir. 1971).

49. *Hailes v. United Air Lines*, 464 F.2d 1006 (5th Cir. 1972); *Diaz v. Pan American Airways*, 442 F.2d 385 (5th Cir. 1971).

50. *Condit v. United Air Lines*, 45 U.S. Law Week 2178 (E.D. Va. 1976).

51. *Dothard v. Rawlinson*, 432 U.S. — 1977.

52. *Richards v. Griffith Rubber Mills*, 300 F. Supp. 338 (D. Ore. 1969).

53. 29 C.F.R. 1604.2.

54. *Keckeisen v. Independent School District*, 509 F.2d 1062 (8th Cir. 1975).

55. *Cleveland Board of Education v. LaFleur*, 414 U.S. 632 (1974).

56. 29 C.F.R. 1604.2.

57. *General Electric Co. v. Gilbert*, 429 U.S. 125 (1976). About a year later, however, the Supreme Court held that an employer may not deprive a female employee of accumulated seniority when she takes an unpaid leave of absence for maternity purposes. *Nashville Gas Co. v. Satty*, 46 U.S. Law Week 4026 (1977).

58. *Brooklyn Union Gas Co. v. New York State Human Rights Appeal Board*, 390 N.Y.S.2d 884, 41 N.Y.2d 84, 359 N.E.2d 393 (1976).

59. *Mieth v. Dothard*, 418 F. Supp. 1169 (M.D. Ala. 1976); cf. *Hardy v. Stumpf*, 37 Cal. App 3d 958, 112 Cal. Rptr. 739 (1974).

60. *Albermarle Paper Co. v. Moody*, 422 U.S. 405 (1975).

61. *Fitzpatrick v. Bitzer*, 427 U.S. 445 (1976).

62. 20 U.S.C. Section 1461 (Supp. 1975); *Cannon v. Northwestern University*, 559 F.2d 1063 (7th Cir. 1977). But cf. *Piascik v. Cleveland Museum of Art*, 426 F. Supp. 779 (N.D. Ohio 1976).

63. *Reeves v. Eaves*, 411 F. Supp. 531 (N.D. Ga. 1976).

64. *Schaeffer v. Tannian*, 538 F.2d 1234 (6th Cir. 1976).

65. *Cramer v. Virginia Commonwealth University*, 415 F. Supp. 673 (E.D. Va. 1976).

66. Ibid., p. 680–81.

67. *Howard v. Ward County*, 418 F. Supp. 494 (D.N.D. 1976), discussing the difference between remedies afforded under Title VII and under the Equal Pay Act.

VII

Procedural Rights of Public Employees

The loss of public employment may come about in many different ways. A person may simply fail to get a job he or she seeks. Once hired, a government worker may be dismissed or discharged. Or a person may be "asked to resign" under circumstances that leave no choice. Sometimes a denial of tenure or a failure to be promoted may have the effect of a discharge. A term appointment or contract may simply not be renewed, or a person may be laid off or suspended for a long period. A position may be phased out or eliminated, causing the displacement of the incumbent. In times of financial stringency for states, cities, towns, and counties, public employees are especially vulnerable because personnel costs comprise the major item in government budgets. Thus it is essential to understand the procedures for termination of public employment.

Moreover, substantive rights may have little value without procedural safeguards. If a government employee may be dismissed without a hearing, there may be no effective way to vindicate a right to free speech, or privacy, or equal opportunity. Even for the person who can afford to file a lawsuit to regain his or her position, the practical chances of success may be slight if the agency is not required to grant any sort of internal hearing. The reasons for the dismissal may be obscure, or even nonexistent, and the employee's ability to assert a constitutional right may thus be effectively defeated.

The purpose of a hearing is not only to vindicate the rights of the individual. The whole system works better if disputes can be adjudicated within an agency. Many conflicts may be capable of early internal resolution, thus avoiding the need for costly and time-consuming resort to the courts. The judicial system, already overburdened, simply could not handle all complaints against administrative agencies, and internal hearings thus become a practical necessity. Hearings also provide a chance for agencies to evaluate or review those on the staff who make and enforce personnel policies. The agency may be helped by internal hearings in revising its own rules. Finally, the confidence of public employees in the fairness of the agencies for which they work may depend heavily on the procedures available for reviewing adverse personnel decisions. For all these reasons, as well as the basic need to protect individual employees' constitutional rights, a hearing system is essential.

Does the law guarantee a hearing to a discharged public employee?

Roughly half of all public employees are covered by Civil Service systems. Most Civil Service laws provide for some sort of hearing in connection with a dismissal or discharge. In the federal Civil Service (which covers 85 percent of all federal employees), the hearing requirement is of long standing. In 1897, President McKinley issued an executive order guaranteeing that no civil servant would be removed "except for just cause and upon written charges of which the accused shall have full notice and an opportunity to make defense."[1] In 1912, these provisions were codified in the Lloyd–La Follette Act, which governs all "adverse actions" by which any employee of the classified service is removed from office, furloughed without pay, suspended for more than 30 days, or reduced in rank or pay.[2] The procedure operates roughly as follows: When an agency wishes to dismiss a staff member, it must give written notice of the proposed action, and invite the employee to reply within 30 days. The agency must also make available to the employee the material on which the charge is based. The employee then has an opportunity to appear before the official vested with authority to make the removal decision in order to answer the charges. The employee may appeal either to the head of the agency or to the Civil Service Commission. If the employee fails to appeal within 30 days, the agency's decision becomes final. If an appeal is taken, the employee is entitled at some stage to a trial-type hearing before a trial examiner, with opportunity for cross-examination and testimony under oath.[3] The major federal agencies have adopted more detailed rules under the Lloyd–La Follette Act, some of which provide more elaborate procedures than others, and may (but need not) provide for a trial-type hearing within the agency.

The time required to follow such procedures may be substantial. According to a recent study, more than 75 percent of adverse actions contested within the employing agency take longer to decide than the 60 days prescribed by Civil Service regulations. Half take more than three months, and 5 percent stay within the agency for over a year. If an employee appeals beyond the agency, another two months may elapse (in a regional office of the Civil Service Commission), and another three months will typically be required before a final decision comes from the commission's Board of Appeals and Review. If the employee then wishes to challenge the decision in court, substantial additional time and expense are involved.

Does the Constitution guarantee a hearing where the statute does not?

The answer to this is complex and confusing. In recent years, the courts have held that many types of government benefits may not be taken away without a prior hearing. A welfare or unemployment compensation recipient may not be taken off the rolls,[4] a state college or university student may not be expelled,[5] a driver's license or a parole may not be revoked,[6] or other benefits terminated without a full hearing.[7] But the Supreme Court has always stopped short of guaranteeing such rights for public employees. Until recently, it was assumed that most government employment could be terminated with only the procedures required by statute.

In a pair of cases in the summer of 1972, the Supreme Court did establish some procedural safeguards. The Court began by recognizing that public employment was not a mere "privilege" that could be granted or withdrawn at the will or whim of an agency head. At the same time, not every termination of public employment required due process. For example, the Court held in *Board of Regents v. Roth*[8] that the simple routine denial of reappointment or the refusal to extend a year-to-year contract of public employment would not require a hearing. The conditions that would demand due process were three: when the dismissal violated an independent constitutional right, such as the employee's freedom of expression; when the dismissal abridged the employee's "property" rights; or when the constitutional interest in "liberty" was violated by the agency action. Otherwise, a public employee could be denied continuing employment or reappointment without a hearing. Thus the procedural protections available to a public employee are narrower than those available to almost any other government beneficiary. In the following sections, we will examine the implications of these decisions.

Does an action that infringes substantive constitutional rights require a hearing?

Yes. In *Perry v. Sindermann*,[9] the Court made clear that government may not fire a person for asserting freedom of expression or some other protected interest. The faculty member involved in that case claimed that his termination resulted from his criticism of policies of the college administration. The trial court had refused to take testimony on this issue, since it felt the professor had no right to a hearing. "Plainly," said the Supreme Court, "these allegations present a bona fide constitutional claim . . . [since] a teacher's public criticism of his superiors on matters of public concern may be constitutionally protected and may, therefore, be an impermissible basis for termination of his employment."[10]

It is not necessary that the agency have announced that the employee's speech was the reason for the termination; a federal court of appeals has recently explained:

> The concurrence of protected speech which may be unpopular with college officials, and the termination of the employment contract seem to be enough, in the view of the Supreme Court, to occasion inquiry to determine whether or not the failure to renew the contract was in fact caused by the protected speech.[11]

Other courts have held that public employees may claim hearings if, for example, they can show that their dismissal came very soon after their designation as a union representative, a bargaining agent, or a member of a new union—even though the employer said nothing about such activity in the termination notice.[12]

This procedural right is not limited to First Amendment or free speech interests. Other constitutional interests may also support claims to procedural due process. For example, as one legal commentary recently observed, "Employees who are members of a racial minority can inevitably get a hearing by claiming that their dismissal was racially motivated."[13] A person who has been discharged in violation of the constitutional right to privacy may also be entitled to a hearing on this basis. Although most of the cases have involved First Amendment interests, the principle is not so limited.

Does the abridgment of an employee's "property" right require a hearing?

Yes. In the *Roth* and *Sindermann* cases, the Supreme Court made clear that a hearing was required where an employee could show a "property" interest in continued employment. A "unilateral expectation" would not be enough. A strong desire to continue in the position would not suffice, even though the employee could show need for the money to support his or her family and could not find another job. There must be "a legitimate claim of entitlement" to the job before the "property" interest comes into play and requires a hearing. The Court explained that the nature and scope of this "property" right are defined by *state* law, since there was no applicable federal or constitutional law principle.

Is a tenured employee protected by the "property" theory?

Yes, clearly so. In fact, long before the *Roth* and *Sindermann* cases, the Supreme Court had held that a tenured university professor could not be discharged without some inquiry into his or her fitness to teach;[14] the 1972 decisions reaffirmed and clarified the due process right as an important incident of tenure.[15]

In the *Sindermann* case, in fact, the Supreme Court went beyond tenure guaranteed by a written contract. An employee who had served a long period, "might be able to show from the circumstances of this service—

and from other relevant facts—that he has a legitimate claim of entitlement to job tenure." The professor in question had alleged that the "policies and practices of the institution" conferred a *de facto* tenure, which the Court held he was entitled to prove as the basis for his procedural claim.

It is also possible that state or local law or agency rules might afford the employee *some* procedural protection—enough to suggest a substantial relationship, and thus imply a property interest—without meeting the standards of constitutional due process. There is an irony in this suggestion: If the agency voluntarily goes part way toward due process, it may be constitutionally required to go the whole way, though any such obligation could have been avoided by being harder-hearted in the beginning.

It is clear that a dismissal of an employee during a contract period—for example, firing a teacher in the middle of an academic year—will give rise to a hearing, since the person has a comparable "property" interest in keeping his or her job through the stated period.[16] The interruption of a term is quite different from the simple failure to renew the appointment at the end of the term.

Do persons with "permanent" jobs have a right to a hearing?

Not necessarily. Most probationary employees have no "property" interest. The 1972 cases did not settle the status of persons who do not have tenure but are classified as "permanent" under state or local law. The Supreme Court squarely faced this issue in the 1976 case of *Bishop v. Wood*,[17] involving the summary discharge of a North Carolina city police officer. Since the officer was classified as "permanent" after three years of satisfactory service, he claimed that he had the kind of "property" interest in a hearing that the Supreme Court had earlier recognized. The Court acknowledged that "on its face the ordinance may fairly be read as conferring such a guarantee." But, it continued, that was not the only possible reading; "the ordinance may also be construed as guaranteeing no right to continued employment but merely conditioning an employee's removal on compliance with certain specified procedures." At this point, the Court deferred to the federal district judge, who presumably knew most about North Carolina law, and who had ruled that the police officer "held his position at the will and the pleasure of the city." Thus, despite the local law, which classified the position as "permanent," and undoubtedly gave city employees an expectation of continued employment, the requisite "property" interest did not exist. Through this recent holding, the Supreme Court has significantly qualified the "property" branch of its *Roth* and *Sindermann* decisions. The impact of *Bishop* on the evolving "property" claim to due process is not yet clear. Several lower courts have nonetheless required hearings on strikingly similar facts, finding that state law still created the essential expectancy, while one court has taken a substantially narrower view of the employee's procedural rights on the basis of *Bishop*.[18] The elaboration of this major new decision will undoubtedly require some time.

Can an employee claim a "property" interest simply through a long term of service?

Only if the term is very long, and even then the claim is doubtful. Several courts have held that satisfactory service, without tenure, for six or eight years, would not suffice to create a "property" claim.[19] One case that seems to reach an opposite conclusion involved a teacher who had taught for 29 years and was then dismissed without a hearing. The court of appeals held that such a person should at least be given a chance to argue that such a period of unblemished service created a "property" interest.[20] In light of the *Bishop* holding that even persons classified as "permanent" may not have a property interest in the job, a claim based simply on length of service now seems doubtful.

Does the infringement of a public employee's "liberty" require a hearing?

Yes. The Supreme Court held in the *Roth* and *Sindermann* cases that a termination might deprive a public employee of "liberty" in either of two ways: Such an action might "seriously damage [the employee's] standing and associations in the community" or it might impose "a stigma or other disability that foreclosed his freedom to take advantage of other employment opportunities."[21] Presumably, under this standard an employee could prove a "liberty" interest through either "the objective consideration of employment deprivation [or] subjective consideration of social stigma." The routine, unexplained nonreappointment would not, however, give rise to a liberty interest any more readily than to a property interest.

The recent cases have indicated that a rather substantial deprivation is required for a liberty claim. For example, courts have held that terminations based on the following charges do not meet this standard: "malfeasance"; noncooperation, display of "anti-establishment obsession"; failure to perform a particular job; failure to meet certain minimum standard requirements; or failure to cooperate with fellow workers.[22] On the other hand, courts have found the following charges to require a hearing because they abridged "liberty": alleged racism, dishonesty and lack of integrity, alleged mental instability, lack of performance, unwillingness to carry out institutional policies, and moral turpitude.[23] As the survey collecting these cases concluded, "The distinction seems less than clear."[24] In deciding whether a particular charge invades the employee's liberty, courts have considered such factors as the level of the position, the employee's age, and the financial impact of the discharge. A court might also consider the degree to which the particular occupation is under government control, since the discharged employee's options are greater where a broad range of private-sector alternatives exist than where government accounts for almost all the available positions.

The Supreme Court has recently introduced an important procedural qualification: The "liberty" interest in a hearing may be lost or forfeited if the employee does not claim it by challenging the truth of the allegedly stigmatizing statements. The purpose of a hearing in such a case, the Court observed in a brief unsigned opinion, is "solely 'to provide the person an opportunity to clear his name.'" The Court then added: "If he does not challenge the substantial truth of the material in question, no hearing would afford a promise of achieving that result for him."[25]

Must the charge be communicated to others in order to deprive the employee of "liberty"?

Yes, in light of the Supreme Court's 1976 decision in *Bishop v. Wood*. The discharged police officer, having lost on his property claim, also argued that his liberty had been abridged—both because the charges given him by the city manager created a stigma and because they were false. The Supreme Court was willing to assume the charges were false, but held that that fact by itself did not violate the officer's liberty interest. The other part of the claim was more difficult. The city manager told the police officer he was being dismissed for failure to follow certain orders, poor attendance at police training classes, causing poor morale, and for other conduct unsuited to an officer. But these charges were not communicated to anyone else at the time of the discharge, and became public only when they were written down in the course of preparing for trial of the lawsuit. The Supreme Court now held that no matter how serious the charges, they could not form the basis of a "liberty" interest (and thus support a due process claim) unless they were made public or conveyed to others.[26] Presumably, the police officer's claim would have been somewhat stronger if before bringing suit he had sought another job and the charges had been divulged to a future employer.

Can a liberty interest arise if no reasons for a dismissal are given?

It is possible that a statute or ordinance would provide for the dismissal of a certain employee only on specific and narrow grounds, any one of which would be "stigmatizing." If such an employee were discharged without a hearing, an inference would arise that one of the stated grounds existed. The employee might be able to argue that his or her "liberty" had been abridged, even though no charges had been given explicitly, if the only fair implication were unmistakenly harmful to his or her reputation and to future employment opportunities. Typically, however, the possible grounds for dismissal are broad enough that such a stigma would not be created by an unexplained termination.

Such a claim could also arise, said the Supreme Court in the *Roth* case, if the unexplained termination severely restricted other employment options—for example, because of a rule barring a professor from teaching at all other state universities. The Court suggested that where a termination, with or without explanation, "foreclose[d] a range of opportunities," a due process claim would arise. On the other hand, the Court held insufficient mere proof that a teacher would be "somewhat less attractive to other employers" after he had been denied reappointment at one university.[27]

What are the elements of "due process" when a hearing is required?

There is no easy or even clear answer to this. The Supreme Court has never spelled out the minimal elements of a public employee's due process. The competing interests of the government agency and the individual employee are likely to be balanced in each case to determine what procedures are constitutionally required, since the Supreme Court has stressed that due process is a flexible concept. A few elements can, however, be identified.

When a hearing is required, the employee is generally entitled to adequate prior notice that gives both time to prepare and sufficient information about the charges so that preparation can be meaningful. At the hearing, the employee must have an opportunity both to present evidence in his or her own behalf and to counter the evidence against him—usually by cross-examination of adverse witnesses. If the employee can afford to retain counsel, the attorney should be allowed to appear and argue at the hearing; on the other hand, due process does not require the agency to provide counsel at public expense. The judgment should rest solely on the evidence adduced at the hearing. The decision maker should be impartial and unbiased, should have the authority to order relief that would meet the employee's needs (back pay, reinstatement, etc.), and should make available to the employee a statement of reasons for the decision. These are the elements of a hearing that some lower courts have required in public employment cases.[28]

Recently, however, the Supreme Court has limited the extent of process due to persons who lose government benefits. The 1976 case of *Mathews v. Eldridge*[29] involved the termination of disability insurance payments. The Court held that the pretermination evidentiary hearing guaranteed to recipients of welfare and unemployment compensation need not be afforded the disabled worker. Throughout the opinion, the Court stressed the "flexibility" of due process, the need to balance individual against institutional interests, the importance of government efficiency and economy, and the acceptability of alternatives to the evidentiary hearing. The majority also found the plight of the disabled worker less compelling than that of the welfare client, who is "on the very margin of subsistence" and has few if any alternative sources of support. Thus the Court held constitutionally adequate a procedure that relied on initial written submissions, followed by pretermination knowledge of the reasons for the action and an opportunity to submit additional arguments and evidence in writing. After termination, the beneficiary could seek an evidentiary, but nonadversary, hearing at which he could be represented by counsel. This procedure, said the Court, would satisfy due process. Moreover, it spared an already burdened agency the costs and other complications of having to give full evidentiary hearings.

The significance of the *Eldridge* case for public employment is unclear. It seems unlikely that the Court would hold that discharged government workers have greater rights than people who lose disability payments. Indeed, the employee will probably fare less well in the future; the Court remarked that "in contrast to the discharged federal employee . . . there is little possibility that the terminated recipient will be able to find even temporary employment to ameliorate the interim loss."[30] This specific reference, together with the Court's declining standard of due process for government beneficiaries, warns that public employees may fare considerably less well than the lower courts have recently treated them if and when the high court reviews the matter of procedures.

Does the public employee have a right to a hearing prior to dismissal or termination?

The regulations of many agencies provide for pretermination hearings. The Supreme Court has held that pretermination hearings are required before welfare, unemployment compensation, and certain other benefits can be taken away. But in other situations, a majority of the Court apparently feels that a posttermination hearing is constitutionally adequate. In the 1974 case of *Arnett v. Kennedy*,[31] some justices would have required a pretermination hearing for all public employees, and others would not have required such a hearing for any public employees. Those in the middle would balance the interests of the government agency against those of the individual and decide whether a pretermination hearing was warranted. In the *Arnett* case, a majority upheld the constitutionality of the Lloyd–La Follette Act, which provides only for an informal appeal prior to termination and guarantees a trial-type hearing only *after* the action becomes effective.

There are, however, some important qualifications. First, if the agency's own rules provide for a pretermination hearing, the guarantee may not be withdrawn or curtailed in individual cases. The Supreme Court has held many times that a government agency is bound to follow its own rules, even where the procedures provided by those rules may not be constitutionally required.[32]

Second, a posttermination hearing would suffice only if the agency provides some opportunity to contest the decision before it becomes effective—at the very least, a chance to know the reasons for the decision and to dispute them before a responsible agency official.[33] (There may, of course, be "emergency" situations, such as that involving strikes by firefighters and police officers, where even such interim procedures as these can be dispensed with in the interests of protecting the public safety.[34])

Third, the posttermination evidentiary hearing must be at a "meaningful" time—that is, very soon after the discharge becomes effective, since a long delay could deny any meaningful relief to the unemployed person.

Fourth, some laws affect the late hearing by providing that the employee who eventually prevails shall be reinstated with back pay and other retroactive benefits. Such a provision is no substitute for a hearing before dismissal, but does at least make the posttermination appeal more attractive.

Finally, the lower courts seem to have been more persuaded by a "liberty" claim than by a "property" interest in deciding whether a pretermination hearing is required. Since the "liberty" cases usually involve an employee's desire to clear his or her name of damaging charges, the courts may feel that here justice requires prompt action more clearly than where the issue is the less emotional one of "entitlement."[35]

Does due process include access to an impartial decision maker?

Yes, but that does not require that the person have had no prior involvement with the case. Courts have universally recognized that due process requires an impartial, unbiased forum. A person who has already made up his or her mind about the case—in one instance, by having hired a permanent replacement for the employee who was appealing—is not able to judge the case objectively. But not every degree of involvement will disqualify a decision maker. Quite recently, the Supreme Court considered the question of whether a school board can impartially review the dismissals of teachers engaged in a strike against the board. The teachers had argued that such a hearing denied them due process for two reasons: (1) because the board had a stake in the outcome of the strike, and (2) because the board was in fact a participant in the negotiations that precipitated the discharge of the striking teachers. The Supreme Court rejected both claims, and held that the board could serve as an impartial hearing body.[36] First, the Court ruled that the school board lacked "the kind of personal and financial stake in the decision that might create a conflict of interest" even though the strike had created some bitterness in the community. The Court also held that "mere familiarity with the facts of a case gained by an agency in the performance of its statutory role does not . . . disqualify a decision maker." Nor, said the majority, is an agency unfairly biased because it has previously taken a public position on the issue involved in the discharge, without proof that it is incapable of judging the particular controversy fairly. Thus, despite the fact that the board had triggered the discharge and that the negotiations were still going on, the Court held that due process had been satisfied.

Several factors in this case may temper the force of the decision. For one thing, the strike was illegal under Wisconsin law, and the substantive issue was thus unusually clear and narrow. Moreover, the state laws gave the school board very explicit powers with respect to both the dismissal of teachers and the management of the school district—powers that in the Supreme Court's view would have been seriously undermined if the board could not act as the hearing body. Also, as a practical matter, there were no obvious alternatives. Even the state Supreme Court, which found the school board biased, could only suggest that the board render an initial decision, subject to review by a court. In the absence of some better alternative designed by the legislature, the state court felt powerless to provide an alternative forum for review of teacher dismissals.

Do the guarantees of due process apply to agency actions short of dismissal?

The answer depends both on the nature of the sanction and on the other circumstances of the case. A forced resignation may, for example, have precisely the effect of a dismissal and give rise to similar procedural rights.[37] On the other hand, many types of milder sanctions will not trigger the full range of due process guarantees, even if a "liberty" or "property" interest is affected. The Supreme Court has not dealt directly with the issue of lesser sanctions. A 1973 case involving a suspension was sent back to a lower court for reconsideration,[38] and a similar case was actually heard by the Supreme Court in 1976 but later remanded after the agency revised its rules to provide for presuspension hearings.[39]

The lower courts have proceeded largely on their own in this area. In cases involving suspensions, even for fairly short terms, public employees have generally been held entitled to a hearing, sometimes even prior to suspension.[40] There are decisions to the contrary, but they seem to be in the minority.[41] Other penalties short of dismissal—for example, certain kinds of lateral transfers—have been held to require a hearing at least where the *Roth-Sindermann* elements are present.[42] An adverse performance rating, which did not deprive the employee of his job but presumably hurt his chances for advancement, has also been found to require a hearing.[43] On the other hand, there are cases involving demotions or removal of employees from administrative or supervisory positions in which hearings have not been mandated. One court found that the summary denial to a federal employee of a security clearance not necessary for his current job was constitutionally proper.[44] Given the range of possible sanctions short of dismissal, it is obviously difficult to generalize. Perhaps the most that can be said is that conscientious courts will balance the agency's interests against those of the individual and fashion procedures accordingly. Undoubtedly, the Supreme Court will consider the issue of lesser sanction sometime soon, since it has twice agreed to consider the constitutionality of summary suspensions.

Is a hearing ever available following an initial denial of employment?

Yes, under rather unusual conditions. Even though the initial applicant generally has fewer rights than the incumbent, one court has required a hearing for a person whose application for public employment was rejected. The person had applied for a secretarial position with a city agency. The application was turned down simply because of "unsatisfactory references." The applicant asked for a hearing, but the agency insisted that the file should remain confidential. When suit was brought, the federal court found that due process entitled the applicant to know the sources and substance of the allegedly damaging references, and to have an opportunity to refute the charges. The court concluded: "All persons, including [the applicant] should have a right to or interest in fair consideration for public employment, including consideration for placement on the eligible civil service list."[45] While an applicant clearly has no "property" interest in public employment, this case indicates that the "liberty" interest may be sufficient even at the initial stage to require a hearing under unusual conditions.

Are some positions in the public service "above" or "beyond" due process?

At certain levels in the public service, courts would be far less inclined to probe the dismissal process. For example, persons holding "policy-making" positions may be dismissed for partisan political reasons, even though the Supreme Court has held that patronage dismissal of routine public employees abridges First Amendment rights.[46] On this basis, a court would probably be less likely to order a hearing in the case of a high-ranking policy maker since the need for personal loyalty and harmony are greatest at this level of the public service.[47] Even at the policy-making level, however, a discharge that either violated a clear property interest or seriously jeopardized an employee's liberty might still require a hearing. The courts have never suggested that people who assume senior positions in the public service must completely abandon their constitutional rights.

If an internal procedure is provided by law, must a discharged employee pursue it before seeking external relief?

In general, yes. Courts usually require that persons complaining of administrative action "exhaust" internal remedies before going outside the agency. There are sound reasons for this rule. The dispute may reflect a minor misunderstanding that can be quickly resolved even through an informal conference. Even where that is not possible, an internal procedure may sharpen the issues and possibly develop a record that will be useful at later stages. The time and expense in going outside the agency are obviously far greater, both for the individual employee and for the agency. And if everyone can bypass the internal procedures with impunity, they may cease to be meaningful even for those who wish to use them. Thus the exhaustion of internal remedies is usually required.

But there is an important exception: The remedy must be adequate to the grievant's needs. If an internal remedy would not have brought redress, then prior recourse to it may not always be required. In one recent federal case, a discharged fireman had gone directly to court, claiming that only a presuspension hearing would protect his constitutional rights. The court of appeals not only upheld the constitutional claim, but also agreed that he had properly bypassed the internal process because of its inadequacy. A 1976 Supreme Court decision allowed a disability insurance claimant to bypass internal procedures because of compelling circumstances; the claimant had "raised a colorable claim that because of his physical condition and dependency upon the disability benefits, an erroneous termination would damage him in a way not recompensable through retroactive payments."[48] The claimant had also raised a basic constitutional claim, which was especially appropriate for resolution in the courts rather than in the very agency whose procedures were being questioned on constitutional grounds.

Such a course is risky, however. If a court later decides that the internal appeal is constitutionally adequate, the employee must then go back to the beginning, having lost substantial time (and probably money as well). Thus it is far wiser to pursue the internal procedures first, unless one is certain that bypassing them is justifiable.

Must the agency follow its own procedures even if they are not constitutionally mandated?

Yes. The Supreme Court has held in several major cases that if the legislature or an agency's own rules guarantee a hearing, the procedure may not be short-circuited even if a hearing is not constitutionally required. Thus the agency may not decide that certain cases are appropriate for full hearing and others are not—for example, because they involve no "liberty" or "property" interests.[49] If the legislature wishes to change the rules, it may do so prospectively and for all cases, but a general requirement may not be dispensed selectively in particular cases.

May the hearing requirements be satisfied by due process in some other proceeding?

One court has held that even where an employee is entitled to a hearing on charges that led to dismissal, that requirement may be satisfied by due process in some other forum. The specific case involved a California school teacher whose certificate was revoked following conviction for a sex offense. After the criminal trial and appeal, the teacher argued that the State Board of Education must also grant a hearing before revoking his certificate. The court upheld the summary procedure, however, on the ground that an opportunity to be fully heard in one forum suffices.[50] This decision is questionable, because the interests of the prosecutor are not precisely those of the state education officials or the local school board. The Courts have held, for example, that a lawyer disbarred by one court may not be automatically disbarred by other courts, since the issues in the second proceeding may not be precisely the same as those in the first. A similar rule should apply to public employment: If a discharged employee is constitutionally entitled to a hearing, that right can be vindicated only by consideration of his or her claims "at a meaningful time and in a meaningful manner"—which would usually require special administrative review.

How does collective bargaining affect procedural rights of public employees?

An agreement between a public employee union and the employer may provide certain remedies and procedures for dismissal (or lesser penalties). The contract will probably also provide that such remedies are exclusive of others afforded by statute or regulations. Both members of the union and of the agency would be bound to follow the contract provisions in the first instance. A discharged employee might, however, still go to court claiming that the contract remedy was constitutionally inadequate. If that claim were sound, the court would probably not hold that the employee had bargained away his constitutional right when the union settled for a less generous procedure. Instead, the collective bargaining agreement would presumably be interpreted in light of preexisting constitutional rights of public employees.

NOTES

1. *15th Report of the United States Civil Service Commission,* p. 70 (1897–98), Rule II.
2. 5 U.S.C. §§ 7501 et seq. (1970).
3. 5 C.F.R. 735.201a sets forth the regulations of the Civil Service Commission; individual agencies also have rules of their own covering such procedural matters.
4. *California Department of Human Resources Development v. Java,* 402 U.S. 121 (1971); *Goldberg v. Kelly,* 397 U.S. 254 (1970).
5. *Dixon v. Alabama State Board of Education,* 294 F.2d 150 (5th Cir. 1961).
6. *Bell v. Burson,* 402 U.S. 535 (1971); *Morrissey v. Brewer,* 408 U.S. 471 (1972).
7. *Fuentes v. Shevin,* 407 U.S. 67 (1972); *Sniadach v. Family Finance Corp.,* 395 U.S. 337 (1969).
8. 408 U.S. 564 (1972).
9. 408 U.S. 593 (1972).
10. Ibid., p. 598.
11. *Chitwood v. Feaster,* 468 F.2d 359, 361 (4th Cir. 1972).

12. *Sarteschi v. Burlein,* 508 F.2d 110 (3rd Cir. 1975); *George v. Conneaut Board of Education,* 472 F.2d 132 (6th Cir. 1972).
13. Note, Due Process Rights of Public Employees, 50 *New York University Law Review* 310, 354 (1975).
14. *Slochower v. Board of Higher Educ.,* 350 U.S. 551 (1956).
15. *Needleman v. Bohlen,* 386 F. Supp. 741 (D. Mass. 1974); *Chung v. Park,* 369 F. Supp. 959 (M.D. Pa. 1974).
16. *Bhargave v. Cloer,* 355 F. Supp. 1143 (N.D. Ga. 1972).
17. 426 U.S. 341 (1976).
18. *Olshock v. Village of Skokie,* 541 F.2d 1254 (7th Cir. 1976); *Berns v. Civil Service Commission,* 537 F.2d 714 (2d Cir. 1976); *Hewitt v. D'Ambrose,* 418 F. Supp. 966 (S.D.N.Y. 1976). One court, however, has found since *Bishop* that state law limiting terminations to "cause" no longer creates a "property" right for hearing purposes. *Banks v. Redevelopment Authority of Philadelphia,* 416 F. Supp. 72 (E.D. Pa. 1976).
19. *Patron v. Howland Local Schools Board of Education,* 472 F.2d 159 (6th Cir. 1972).
20. *Johnson v. Fraley,* 470 F.2d 179 (4th Cir. 1972).
21. *Roth v. Board of Regents,* 408 U.S. 564, 573 (1972).
22. *Adams v. Walker,* 492 F.2d 1003 (7th Cir. 1974).
23. *Willner v. Minnesota State Junior College Board,* 487 F.2d 153 (8th Cir. 1973); *Churchwell v. United States,* 414 F. Supp. 499 (D.S.D. 1976).
24. Note, Due Process Rights of Public Employees, 50 *New York Law Review* 310, 333 (1975).
25. *Codd v. Velger,* 429 U.S. 624 (1977).
26. 426 U.S. 341 (1976).
27. 408 U.S. at 574, n. 13.
28. *Hostrop v. Board of Junior Colleges,* 471 F.2d 488 (7th Cir. 1972).
29. 424 U.S. 319 (1976).
30. Ibid., p. 341.
31. 416 U.S. 134 (1974).
32. *Vitarelli v. Seaton,* 359 U.S. 535 (1959).
33. Compare *Behan v. City of Dover,* 419 F. Supp. 562 (D. Del. 1976), suggesting that actual knowledge may sometimes suffice in place of formal notice.
34. *Olshock v. Village of Skokie,* 411 F. Supp. 257, 264 (N.D. Ill. 1976).
35. *Churchwell v. United States,* 414 F. Supp. 499, 503 (D.S.D. 1976).
36. *Hortonville Joint School District No. 1 v. Hortonville Education Association,* 426 U.S. 482 (1976).
37. *Battle v. Mulholland,* 439 F. 2d 321. (5th Cir. 1971).
38. *Snead v. Civil Service Commission,* 355 F. Supp. 764

(S.D.N.Y. 1973), 389 F. Supp. 935 (S.D.N.Y.), *vacated and remanded*, 421 U.S. 982 (1975).

39. *Muscare v. Quinn*, 520 F.2d 1212 (7th Cir. 1975), *vacated*, 425 U.S. 560 (1976).

40. *Buggs v. City of Minneapolis*, 358 F. Supp. 1340 (D. Minn. 1973).

41. *McIntyre v. New York Department of Corrections*, 411 F. Supp. 1257 (S.D.N.Y. 1976).

42. *Adock v. Board of Education*, 109 Cal. Rptr. 676, 513 P.2d 900 (1973).

43. *Bottcher v. Florida Department of Agriculture and Consumer Services*, 365 F. Supp. 1123 (N.D. Fla. 1973).

44. *Finley v. Hampton*, 473 F.2d 180 (D.C. Cir. 1972).

45. *Norlander v. Schleck*, 345 F. Supp. 595 (D. Minn. 1972).

46. *Elrod v. Burns*, 427 U.S. 347 (1976).

47. *Jaffree v. Scott*, 372 F. Supp. 264 (N.D. Ill. 1974).

48. *Mathews v. Eldridge*, 424 U.S. 319 (1976).

49. *Vitarelli v. Seaton*, 359 U.S. 535 (1959).

50. *Purifoy v. State Board of Education*, 30 Cal. App. 3rd 187, 106 Cal. Rptr. 201 (1973).